VANDALS IN THE GARDEN

BY PETE PERRY

AN ANTHOLOGY OF MANKIND'S DESTRUCTION

This book is not for the squeamish. You will never regard the human race in the same light again!

The follow-up to
'This Garden Earth'

VANDALS IN THE GARDEN

ISBN: 1 903607 75 2
978 1 903607 75 6

Published by:

Able Publishing
13 Station Road
Knebworth
Herts SG3 6AP

Tel: 01438 812320 / 814316
Fax: 01438 815232
Email: **books@able publishing.co.uk**

www.ablepublishing.co.uk

VANDALS IN THE GARDEN

Contents

ACKNOWLEDGMENTS

The following works of reference and individuals were used in the writing of this book …

Life on Earth, David Attenborough Productions Ltd., 1979
The Living Planet, David Attenborough Productions Ltd., 1984
Knowledge, Purnell & Sons Ltd., 1968
The Book of Knowledge, The Waverley Book Co. Ltd., 1958
Quest, Marshall Cavendish Ltd., 1990
Bury my heart at Wounded Knee, written by Dee Brown, published by Barrie & Jenkins Ltd., 1970
Earth in Upheaval, written by Immanuel Velicovsky, published by Sidgewick & Jackson Ltd., 1956
Microsoft Encarta '95
British Daily Newspapers, British television and radio news items, 1967 - 1998

PERSONAL ACKNOWLEDGEMENTS

Special thanks to Jill Sawyer for the use of books from her library and for correcting and typing out the original manuscript; to Frank Swaine for additional information and for keeping my computer updated and running smoothly; to Les Prickett and John Abbey for their lively debates on environmental matters; to Shirley and my children, Vivien, Deborah, Sean, Corina, Tania and Michael for additional information and for taking such a keen interest; and finally, a very special thank you to Jon Ridley who helped with my research. And more especially to Jon's wife (at the time) Jill, who went through the laborious task of typing out the first draft. Thanks also to Paul Foot for his honest reporting, for which he lost his job!

INTRODUCTION

In *This Garden Earth*, published in 2005, we discussed how life first formed, and how plants dominated the planet. This gave rise to an oxygen-rich atmosphere, which was detrimental to the plants.

Animals evolved in order to convert the oxygen back into carbon dioxide, for the sake of plant life. The animals not only took advantage of the life-giving gas, but also the lush vegetation upon which they grazed. We saw how life on Earth battled constantly against many natural changes within the environment, and how both plants and animals adapted to meet these challenges.

Mankind finally entered the arena, firstly, following his instincts to work *with* nature, and then, following his selfish streak, working *against* the planet's natural cycle.

We also studied the complexity of the Plant Kingdom, explaining that plants, as well as animals, can reason, and have 'emotions' and physical feelings. This poses a problem for vegetarians and vegans. If it is deemed to be cruel to eat the flesh of animals because they have feelings and emotions like us, is it any *less* cruel to eat *plants?*

Any living creature, whether they be animal or

Pete - Italy

5

plant, thrives and survives upon the biological remains of other creatures. Plants (which are far older than animals) have actually *accepted* this fact of life and produce the only biological by-product on Earth that is actually *designed for eating—fruit*. Indeed, plants *rely* upon other creatures eating their fruit in order for them to distribute the seed and thus continue their genetic line.

In this *second* book, we examine in more detail, how Mankind deviated from being the Earth's natural 'caretakers' to becoming, quite literally, the *Vandals in the Garden...*

Illustrations by the author.
Additional photographs by Chris Taylor and Nikki Heydon.

CHAPTER ONE:
ALLIANCE

From the beginning of life on *This Garden Earth*, different species of plant and animal life have found it to their mutual advantage to live in close proximity with each other. Some have even created *colonies* of related, or even *non-related* species. Indeed, some of the earliest of the land plants, *lichens*, are made up of both *algal* and *fungal* cells, working together in one tight-knit community.

Insects, fish, birds and animals all help in the fertilization and distribution of plants, as well as Mankind's use of the protective, or hunting abilities of other species. Many scavengers, such as hyenas, jackals and vultures actually stay within close proximity of powerful hunters such as lions, cheetahs and leopards in order to grab a quick meal from the spoils. Occasionally, they may even *steal them*!

In the beginning Mankind's hunting skills attracted similar 'hanger's-on'. Mankind was never one of the *largest, strongest*, nor *fastest* of hunters, so he had to rely on cunning, invention and organization. This way he was able to trap and kill animals much larger, stronger and faster than himself in order to feed and clothe his tribe. These skills came from his superior intelligence and his dexterous hands. His opposing thumbs allowed him to make hunting weapons such as crude spears, knives and axes. He was also able to construct traps in which to snare his prey. Add to this the social behaviour of Mankind in living in well-organised tribes and you have the makings of very successful hunters, despite his obvious *physical* shortcomings. Being *smaller, less powerful* and *slower* than most of his prey, he would *startle* his quarry into panic and confusion by shouting and beating bushes. With military precision he would drive the confused animal into a trap, such as a pit covered with branches and leaves. Once the unfortunate animal was ensnared in this way, members of the tribe would throw spears at it until it was dead. Mankind remains the only animal capable of killing other species from a safe distance. Before the invention of the *spear,* it is likely that men would simply throw large *stones* and *rocks* at the poor creature! The result would be fresh meat for the whole tribe, skins for clothing and bones and horns that could be fashioned into tools and implements such as drinking vessels.

Eating the meat 'on site' however, was not an option. Any marauding animals could have stolen the spoils, or even worse, they could have killed the hunters! Besides the carcass was to be shared with mates and children back at the cave. To get the carcass actually back to 'home base', however, was perilous in *itself!* Until the discovery of fire, early humans probably kept the competition at bay by pelting them with stones or threatening them with spears.

Once the power of fire was discovered however, the task became much simpler! All animals, apart from Mankind, are afraid of fire. They do not understand its nature. It is not solid—they cannot attack it. All they know is that it can destroy all forms of life. Mankind learned, probably by trial and error, that fire could also be *useful.* It could be used to scare away other animals and it could be used to cook meat, making it more tender. With these skills and knowledge the tribesmen, carrying the carcass back home, would be flanked by men carrying flaming pieces of wood. Any animal with designs upon stealing the meat would, in this way, be kept at bay, leaving the transportation pathway clear. Once safely inside the cave the carcass would be taken past the fire at the entrance, which was kept constantly alight. This fire served several purposes. It kept marauding animals at bay; it kept the tribe warm during cold periods; it provided light and it was used for cooking the meat.

Cooking was achieved at first by simply throwing the meat into the fire and raking it out again once it was cooked. Later however, the carcass would be suspended over the fire from the roof of the cave. Later still, crude barbecue spits were fashioned from stone and bone.

From the discovery of remains in Stone Age caves, it is quite likely that the huge tusks of mammoths and mastodons were used for this purpose, as many of these tusks measured an incredible ten feet in length.

Indeed, it is quite probable that these huge prehistoric elephants were the first creatures to be made totally extinct, some 30,000 years ago, by Mankind's direct influence. Although mammoths measured some fourteen feet at the shoulder they were very docile, feeding as they did upon vegetation. This made them easy prey for the human hunters. Tribes would trap and kill these magnificent creatures for their meat, their woolly fur and their tusks. The modern day obsession with ivory probably comes from these early beginnings.

There were, however, some animals, that *would* follow the humans back to their caves. They would sit outside, hoping for some leftovers. These were the wolves and wild dogs who were almost as cunning as Mankind himself.

European Wolf

Because Man was not by design a carnivore, he had to cook his meat in order to chew and digest it. Even when cooked there were parts, such as bone, gristle and the entrails, which were totally indigestible to him. Sometimes, there would also be some left over meat, which could not be eaten before it began to go off. Some of the bones were used for making tools, implements and weapons. They were also deliberately cracked open in order to get at the succulent 'bone marrow', the proteins of which were thought to have helped Man's brain to develop. The furs were used for clothing, coverings for the cave floor and for covers during the night. Other parts of the carcass however, had to be discarded before it began to rot and smell. Stone Age Man knew instinctively that if these were left on the floor of the cave, not only would they make movement difficult, by cluttering up the cave, but they would also attract annoying flies and vermin.

Cave people wouldn't have known about the spread of disease via flies and vermin, and yet instinctively they would have known that these things could cause problems. What better way of disposing of waste than by throwing it to the dogs? These people didn't try to keep the wolf *from* the door—they actually *encouraged* it! Hence, about 12,000 years ago, the long-lasting partnership between man and dog began. Even so, it was an uneasy alliance. The canines were encouraged to join the tribes in their hunting expeditions, but were kept from the carcass by the 'torch bearers'. The dogs stuck by the humans however, as they knew that in the end they would be thrown a few scraps after the humans had had their fill. Gradually Mankind realised that such an alliance with the dogs could work to his advantage. The dogs, with their superior sense of smell, could track down a likely quarry and lead the humans to it. Indeed, the dogs might well have *killed* the prey, or at least *held on* to it so that the men could finish it off with their spears. Again, the dogs could easily be scared away from their kill by the men with the fire torches.

So it was that Mankind, using his skills and intelligence, discovered that he could dominate other animals and force them into submission. Eventually these accompanying packs of dogs came to accept the fact that the humans were the dominant force. As long as they got their share of the spoils however, they were quite content with the arrangement. In this way the dogs became a part of the tribe, and even began to protect their masters against aggressors. This was to their benefit, as the humans had become their 'meal ticket'! It is very likely that when a bitch gave birth to a litter of puppies the womenfolk would assist in the delivery, as they would with their own kind, and help in raising the puppies. Once the pups began to be raised in the cave they became 'playmates' for the human children. In this way the dogs became not only useful hunting allies, but also pets. It appears that tribes in various parts of the world also began to domesticate wild *cats* in much the same way.

In Europe, some 8,000 years ago, nomadic tribes learned to follow great herds of wild cattle known as aurochs. Aurochs were certainly not gentle creatures by any means. They were highly aggressive and stood about 2 metres at the shoulder. For this reason they were not easily domesticated. However, the nomadic tribesmen would follow these great beasts on their constant search for grazing ground and watering holes. No doubt their hunting dogs accompanied many of the tribesmen. The dogs would have helped a great deal in controlling the herds and also by *killing* one when necessary. These huge bovines would have supplied plenty of meat for the tribe and dogs alike. They could also supply them with clothing made from the hides (an early form of leather) and the massive horns supplied drinking vessels. Indeed, they supplied the tribes with everything they needed, just as the mammoths had before they became extinct.

Centuries later the American Plains Indians (now known as Native Americans), were still following the same practice by following the great herds of bison which roamed that continent. Indeed, the nomadic tribes of Lapland *still* follow herds of wild reindeer, basing their entire livelihood around the animals—but more about that later.

The early nomadic European tribes soon came to realise that when a cow calved it produced *milk*. The humans found this to be

North American Bison

tasty and nourishing. They also discovered that, once a cow had calved, it would continue to produce milk if milked regularly. Early dairy farming had been discovered! They also discovered that *smaller* bulls and cows were easier to handle. These were often the 'runts', which the herd would normally ignore or abandon in favour of larger, stronger calves. Left to nature, these 'runts' would, as often as not, perish. They very often happened to be albino or piebald (black and white), due to some minor genetic defect.

Aurochs were normally black, so the white or piebald varieties were prey for wolves and other predators—the lighter colour making them easier targets. This, to scientists, is known as natural selection, ensuring that only the fittest animals survive. The tribes however, would take it upon themselves to rear these calves themselves, using milk obtained from the cows. There were many reasons for this. Firstly, as I have already said, they were often smaller and more docile. Also, merely because they were of a different colour, Man has always been attracted to anything 'outside the norm'. Indeed, many prehistoric humans regarded these as sacred, or as a gift from some all-powerful being. And, in separating these white and piebald animals from the main herd, early man had unwittingly discovered selective breeding. He had also begun to upset nature's plan of natural selection. This was the beginning of *livestock farming*. The last truly wild aurochs became extinct in Poland only 300 years ago, and are now known only through fossilised bones.

Some 1,000 years ago European migrants arrived in the Arctic, where they came across vast herds of reindeer. In much the same way as their predecessors, these travellers took to a nomadic existence, following the reindeer herds and treating them in a similar way to their European cousins with the aurochs. The main difference was that, whereas the European tribes had begun selective breeding, eventually leading to cattle farms, the northerners, or Lapps, were quite content to carry on with their nomadic existence. They followed the herds as they grazed, using them for meat, clothing and as beasts of burden.

Elsewhere in 'This Garden Earth', other tribes were beginning to domesticate wild sheep, goats and pigs. Indeed, *pigs* appear to have been among the first animals to be kept as *livestock* and are known to have been domesticated in Thailand since 10,000 BC! Eventually Mankind was keeping a wide variety of livestock, hunting dogs and pet cats— which could keep vermin, such as rats, away from their food.

In much the same way that Mankind was beginning to raise and breed animals for his own purposes, so he began to turn his attention to the *plants* around him. Wild grass seed had long been a part of the diet of early man, as had the roots of vegetables such as wild carrot, sea beet and the potato, as well as wild fruits and nuts. Indeed, it is quite probable that Man was originally an herbivore, as he doesn't possess the teeth nor the digestive system for raw meat!

As with the carcasses of animals, it was more convenient for them to gather these plants from the wild and transport them back to the cave, where they could be shared out with the whole tribe. As for the grasses, it made sense for them to transport the complete seed-heads back, rather than waste time (and risk being attacked) by emptying the husks of seed. Once back at the cave they would empty the husks onto the ground. As we discussed in *This Garden Earth*, the humans, just like the other animals, were doing exactly what the plants *wanted* them to do—distributing their seeds!

With a keen eye on a substantial meal, the gatherers (usually the women-folk and children) would naturally select the largest seeds. Of course, many of these seeds would fall to the ground outside the cave, and begin to germinate. The realisation that these grasses (wheat, barley, corn, rye and, in the case of the Eastern countries, rice) could be raised from seed near their cave had a great effect upon the human race. It made sense for the humans to actually *sow the seeds around their dwelling*. In this way, the cereal crops could be harvested within the safety of their own territory. Since only the largest of the grain was used, Mankind had now unwittingly begun the process of selective breeding in plants as well as in animals.

They soon realised that if *cereal crops* could be grown in the safety of their own environment, then so could *other* plants with culinary, medicinal and *artistic* potential. For some time the cave dwellers had taken to painting scenes, from their life, upon the interior walls. They found that they could make crude paints from coloured clay and from the leaves and petals of plants. Some also used these paints upon their bodies as camouflage; religious symbolism; to strike terror in their enemies; to identify themselves from other tribes; or merely for decorative purposes.

Very soon many tribes were raising crops and livestock within their own territory. Farming had arrived. In order to grow everything they needed however, Mankind found it necessary to increase his territory. He began to clear the great forests. He found, by chopping down the trees, that the vast amounts of wood could be used for *building*. He deserted the old caves and began to build wooden huts to house the increasing numbers in his tribe, as well as making wooden fences to keep their domesticated animals from roaming off. More wood was used later to build great stockades to keep out unwanted and dangerous animals and, it has to be said, unwanted 'neighbours'! In this way, more permanent settlements or 'villages' began to spring up.

The first *town* appears to have sprung up in Jericho, 9,500 years ago. Mankind had become the first animal ever to change drastically the environment around him—with devastating results…

CHAPTER TWO:
THE DESTRUCTION BEGINS...

The clearing and subsequent destruction of forests and woodland to make way for homesteads and farmland gradually spread from the Middle East, almost 10,000 years ago, into Europe and Britain. The British Isles, ten thousand years ago, was completely covered with woodland and great forests.

Here, as in other parts of Europe, Mankind discovered that the wild pigs which inhabited the forests were not only good to eat, but they also had hides that could be used for clothing and shelter from the rain. In fact, every part of the wild boar could be used. So, with the help of his dogs, Mankind found it easy to slaughter these animals for his own needs.

Like the aurochs, he discovered that certain mutants of the wild pig were more docile. Again, these were often smaller, less hairy,

European wild boar

different in colour and the mutant boars often had underdeveloped tusks. This, of course, made them less dangerous. The pigs were added to Mankind's personal selective breeding programme and they joined the other farm animals. Apart from the wild pigs Mankind also hunted deer, elk, reindeer, beavers, bears and wolves with such vigour that their numbers declined dramatically and many species became totally extinct in this country.

The farming tribes of Europe arrived in the south of England about 5,500 years ago, bringing with them their domesticated cattle, goats and sheep, as well as the seeds of cultivated cereal crops and other food plants. Like the rest of Europe, space had to be made for homesteads and farmland. More trees were cut down for this purpose. They also deemed it necessary to clear great tracts of woodland in order to make meadows for their grazing animals, and for mud track roads. The wholesale slaughter of the forests of Britain had begun.

Once these imported animals began to graze, there was little chance of any tree sapling surviving to maturity. Whilst these saplings were young and tender the animals would eat them. The pastures were here to stay! So it was that the landscape of Britain was being changed forever from acres of great forests, to acres of meadow and pastureland. Where once grew massive oaks, elms, limes, beeches and birch, there were now vast fields of crops and grassy meadows. Naturally nature took advantage of these changes, for Mankind had unwittingly created the ideal environment for meadow plants. Cowslips, daisies, buttercups, dandelions and field poppies grew abundantly. But this was to the detriment of many woodland plants. As man cleared the forests for his own purposes, so many of the native flora and fauna became isolated or totally extinct.

Some, such as the oxlip, so treasured by Shakespeare and often mentioned in his works, is now to be found in less than half-a-dozen ancient wet woodlands in East Anglia. The lady's slipper orchid, *Cyprepedium calceolus*, which was also once quite common, is now located in just *one* secret place in Northamptonshire. The red deer and red squirrel retreated northwards as Mankind began to change the landscape, whilst the beaver, bear, elk and reindeer were slaughtered to extinction. The very last boar was killed in Britain in the sixteenth century, as was the last British wolf. In Norfolk there were originally acres of wet woodland full of oxlips and primroses. There were peat bogs, which were home to thriving colonies of butterwort, sundew, mosses and a host of other bog-loving plants. Like other environments, the trees were cut down for space and building materials. The peat bogs were plundered for use as cheap, local fuel and, later, as a soil conditioner for the farmlands. The results of all this human activity were vast trenches and pits, which naturally filled with water. This gave rise to the canals we are so familiar with today, when it was realised that the resulting waterways could be used for the transportation of peat and farm produce. These reed-lined canals have, admittedly, attracted other forms of wildlife, but sadly, at the expense of other flora and fauna. Ironically, conservationists today are busy trying to preserve these habitats, which were originally the result of Mankind's interference!

Likewise, the Scottish highlands were once covered in massive pine forests—the original Caledonian Forest, where red deer, pine martin and wildcat thrived. As recently as 200 years ago, much of this forestland was cleared, not for homesteads, nor indeed for farmland, but for the formation of *heathland and grouse moors!* The cultivation of heather in Scotland was actually encouraged by the gentry of the day, at the expense of other indigenous species of flora and fauna. It was planted specifically for the 'sport' of grouse shooting. Heather provided food and cover for the grouse, merely so that they could breed and hide, to give more 'sport' to the bloodlust of the gentry. Once again, Mankind had changed the environment to suit his own selfish needs, at the expense of other life forms.

Man also introduced the *rabbit* to Britain via Europe (from the Mediterranean) in the eleventh century. It was purposely introduced for the value of its fur and meat. Within two hundred years it had become the commonest medium-sized quadruped in the country. It largely replaced the native British *hares*, of which there were three distinct species. The *mountain hare* now exists only in Scotland and Wales, whilst the *Irish hare*, as the name suggests, can only be found in the Emerald Isles. The most common, although becoming increasingly rare, is the *brown hare*. It is a sad reflection upon Mankind that the hares of Britain are gradually being replaced by rabbits (of which there is only one true species). Previous to the introduction of the rabbit, the three species of hare had led a fairly peaceful existence in the British Isles since the last glacial epoch, some twenty thousand years ago.

Other introductions from foreign parts include pheasants, which were brought over from China and the Caucasus just prior to the Norman invasion. The only reason these have not had a diverse effect upon our native grouse is the fact that *all* 'game' birds have been encouraged to thrive. *Not,* unfortunately, for *environmental* or *conservation* reasons, but to enable the 'gentry' to carry on with their blood sports.

Red fox

For much the same reasons the British *fox* still thrives at the expense of the British *wolf.* If it had been left to the farmers, the red fox would have long become extinct in the British Isles. Because, however, it was considered 'jolly good sport' to chase these creatures around the countryside on horseback with a pack of baying hounds, it has been protected, and, indeed, *bred*, by the very people who *hunt* it! When huntsmen tell you they have to hunt it in order to control its numbers, don't you believe it! In theory, hunting with hounds is now, supposedly, illegal, but try telling the *huntsmen* that! The poor *wolf,* on the other hand, was considered far too large and dangerous for *sporting* purposes! Hunting defenceless animals is deemed good sport, whereas hunting animals that might fight back, is *not*! Typical of the cowards who call themselves 'sporting types'! Add to this the fact that the wolf, in search of a meal, would naturally attack large livestock such as sheep and cattle, you can see why man granted himself the right to exterminate it—it did not fit in with his own, selfish, lifestyle!

Not content with destroying Britain's natural forests and woodlands, Mankind then began to build a totally synthetic environment for himself, once again, at the expense of all other life around him.

As we mentioned earlier, the first true *town* appeared in Jericho 9,500 years ago, although prior to that there were several smaller settlements. The reason for this development was because, by now, Mankind no longer had to go in search of food. He could settle in one place with his livestock and crops close at hand. Safely protected from wild animals he began to breed profusely. As Man's population grew, so did his settlements. Eventually communities were made up of several thousand people.

Walking was laborious and dangerous, what with wild animals on the prowl. So, to enable people from different communities to visit each other, either for social reasons or for trading, some form of transport had to be devised. After all, every predatory animal was much faster on foot than a human being! The horse, which had spread from North America into Europe, Asia and Africa, proved to be the ideal riding animal. It was large, fast and had plenty of stamina. Strangely enough, the Native American species seems to have died out, probably through disease. They were re-introduced by the first human settlers—but more about that later.

Horses appear to have first been used for riding purposes during the bronze-age. Prior to this, they were killed and eaten, so it is likely that, once again, Mankind was responsible for the near extinction of the truly wild horse. The only exceptions to this are the striped horses of Africa, the zebra and quagga, the African wild ass, and the asses of Asia, the kiang and onager. None of these are *true horses* and are not suitable for riding. The last truly wild horse was *Przhesvalski's horse*, which is now extinct as a truly wild species. All other apparently 'wild' herds are escapees from domestic horses. As Mankind began to domesticate the horse, it was soon discovered that it was not only admirably suitable for riding, but could also be used as a beast of burden, pulling carts and later, carriages. It could be used singly, or in harness as teams, to transport not only people, but also luggage and items of trade. They could also be used for pulling ploughs in the field.

Meanwhile in the desert regions of Asia and North Africa the nomadic tribes had found another animal, which could serve a similar purpose to the horse. The dromedary, or Arabian camel, unlike its equine counterpart in Europe, was well adapted to life in the hot dry deserts of Asia and North Africa. It has wide, two-toed feet, which do not sink into the sand. It also has nostrils that can be closed during sandstorms, fat supplies stored in its hump for long journeys without food and a large stomach, which is capable of storing large quantities of water. The dromedaries, (one-humped camels) of the Taureq tribes, have now become completely domesticated. There are *no* wild dromedaries left. The bactrian (two-humped camel) was used for the same purpose by the people of the Steppes and semi-desert regions of Central Asia to Mongolia and northwest to China. There are fewer than 1,000 bactrian camels left in the wild. Apart from acting as beasts of burden, the camels also provided flesh and milk for food, whilst the hides were used to make leather. The long hair of camels is shed every summer and, even today, this is used to make cordage, fine paintbrushes and a light, warm, napped cloth.

4,000 years ago, the people of the Peruvian and Bolivian Andes had already found their own version of the horse and camel. They began to domesticate the wild *guanaco* as a beast of burden. Thousands of years of selective breeding have produced the *llama* that we know today. Although used as a pack animal, the llama, unlike the horse and camel, was never used for riding. Neither was it ever used to pull carts, as the ancient Peruvians and Bolivians never invented the wheel! Like the camel, llamas are sure-footed animals, and have amazing stamina. They can carry as much as 91Kg for twelve hours a day. Unfortunately, for their masters, they are also stubborn like the ass.

When they become weary or are overladen, they will simply lie down and refuse to budge. They have even been known to *spit at their drivers* in protest!

Female llamas are killed for their meat once they are past the fertility stage. Llama meat tastes somewhat like mutton. *Male* llama meat is never eaten, as it is too tough. Llama *milk* is also used extensively throughout west South America. Like the camel, reindeer and the North American bison, llamas provide much of the needs of the human. Llama *wool* is used for the weaving of textiles and the *hides* are tanned for leather, while llama *tallow* is used for making candles. The long *hair* is used for the making of rope and even the *excrement* is not wasted—that is dried and used for fuel, like peat!

Not content with travelling across the *land*, Mankind cast his eyes towards the seas and oceans after he discovered he could travel across water. It all began when he found that he could travel across lakes and rivers upon floating logs. This led to the invention of the canoe, which was originally simply a floating log with one side channelled out for sitting in. More trees were cut down for this purpose. As his skills grew, he began to build craft of a larger and more substantial nature. He discovered that the skins of animals, when hung to upright beams, would catch the wind and propel the craft along—sailing ships had arrived. With these sailing crafts Man could now travel across seas and oceans; settle in different lands; meet different tribes; discover new animals and plants—and proceed to destroy them! It was discovered that these natives of new lands had domesticated their own animals and cultivated different crops. In this way, imports and exports began in a crude fashion.

The Incas of the Andes had cultivated the *potato,* whilst the Aztecs in Mexico had cultivated *runner beans, tomatoes* and *sweetcorn*. The Chinese had developed *rice* and a good culinary *rhubarb*, whilst the Persians were growing *spinach. Carrots* were eaten in Europe, including Britain, but these were the *wild* variety—white-rooted and not very appetising. The *red* form was developed in Afghanistan, whilst *cauliflowers* were cultivated in the Middle East. In Britain the indigenous seaside beet, *beta vulgaris*, was developed into different forms, giving rise to the varieties, *mangle worzles*, *beetroot*, *leaf beet* and *sugar beet*. The Spaniards did not introduce *potatoes* into Europe until 1570, reaching Britain in 1586. It was *Sir Francis Drake* who brought them from the West Indies, where the Spaniards had already established them. Strange, when you think he *could* have got them straight from Spain, if it hadn't been for hostilities between the two nations! *Sir Walter Raleigh* took them across to Ireland, where they became the staple diet of the Irish and a large contributor of the Irish economy. In 1845, Ireland suffered the potato famine, caused by potato blight. It was not until the mainland of England realised what an important food it was, that it became, together with wheat, the staple diet of the English.

No longer was Mankind solely dependent upon wild animals and wild plants for his existence. He could now grow a large selection of flowers, fruit and vegetables and he could raise a large variety of animals for food, clothing, milk and even transport.

Human settlements grew into villages, then into towns, and eventually, into cities. All this time, in the name of 'progress', Mankind was changing the environment around him, solely for his own selfish ends. Natural habitats were declining even more rapidly, as more and more animals and plants became threatened with extinction. Once Mankind began to leave his native shores to explore other lands, the wholesale destruction of life upon 'This Garden Earth' went from bad to worse…

CHAPTER THREE:
NEW LANDS, NEW DESTRUCTION

In the fifteenth century AD the Portuguese landed on the island of Mauritius in the Indian Ocean. They brought with them seeds from their own crops, together with a selection of their own domesticated animals. This, in itself, was to prove disastrous for the ecological balance of the island and was the direct cause of one of the most dramatic and well-known cases of extinction.

Because of the island's lack of predatory animals, a pigeon-like bird, which had lost the use of its wings, had developed there. This bird had never experienced any natural threats to its existence, so there was no need for it to waste any energy in flight. It would forage on the ground for food and so became plump and docile. Its body feathers had become soft and downy and it grew to the size of a large turkey. Due to its trusting nature, the Portuguese sailors named it 'doudo', which, in Portuguese, means 'simpleton'. What the sailors mistook for idiocy was merely a benign nature and that proved to be the bird's downfall. On its native island it had very little to fear, for there had never been any threat to its existence. So trusting were these charming creatures that the Portuguese sailors could simply walk up to it, hit it over the head with a club and kill it for food. Dodos, as they became better known, were good to eat on account of their plumpness. It was like having turkey every day—a real treat for the sailors, who had been living on ship's rations for months!

As more people began to colonise the island of Mauritius the wholesale slaughter of the dodo began. Man's introduction of domestic animals added *further* to their demise. *Pigs* took a liking to dodo eggs, which were, again because of the lack of natural predators, simply laid in a hole on the ground. *Cats* and *dogs*, like the sailors, *also* found the birds to be easy prey. By the end of the seventeenth century, less

Dodo

than 200 years after the first humans arrived on the island, the dodo had become totally extinct.

On the neighbouring islands of Reunion and Rodriguez two *other* species, similar to the dodo, existed. They were very similar in size, but had longer necks and a less awkward gait when they walked. From historical records these birds appeared to be two distinct species. Because they appeared to prefer foraging around alone in the forests, however, the European seamen, who first discovered them, called both species *solitaires*. Like the dodo, they had no natural enemies on their islands, so they were not afraid of the sailors when they landed. Solitaires too became totally extinct by the end of the eighteenth century.

On all three islands there also lived giant tortoises, which grew to a length of over a metre and weighed up to 200 kilos. Similar species of tortoise also lived on the Comono Islands and also in Madagascar. Because of their slow-moving lifestyle, they too, were easy prey for the sailors. They would be taken alive to the ships and killed during the voyage to provide fresh meat for the crew. A large cumbersome

Solitaire

24

creature such as the tortoise could not possibly escape from the hold of the ship, so it made sense to keep them alive until they were required for meat. Apart from a few specimens still thriving upon the island of Aldabra (a part of the Seychelles), the giant tortoise had virtually been exterminated by Mankind by the end of the nineteenth century. The only reason those living on Aldabra had survived was because the islands are so isolated. They were so far from the main shipping routes of the time that humans rarely ventured there. Happily, there are now an estimated 150,000 giant tortoises now living on the Seychelles.

Long before *Christopher Columbus* crossed the Atlantic, Polynesians made great journeys across the oceans in their immense double-hulled craft. The Polynesians sailed to the mainland of Asia to the Marquesas. From there they travelled *north* to Hawaii, *west* to Tahiti, *east* to the Easter islands and eventually they travelled the 4,000 kilometres to New Zealand. The last wave of voyagers settled in New Zealand about 1150 AD. Here, in the two islands of New Zealand, they discovered a strange land inhabited by strange species of plants and animals, some of which existed nowhere else on 'This Garden Earth'. Even today, there are about 1,500 species of plants that grow nowhere else in the world. New Zealand, like Australia, had been cut off from the rest of the world for millions of years. In some respects it had been frozen in time.

Because the Polynesian crafts were so huge, they carried with them hundreds of passengers, male and female. In their holds they carried the roots and seeds of many different kinds of food-plants, as well as domesticated animals and various *other* commodities, which they considered essential, in order to make permanent settlements. The main reason for taking livestock such as pigs and chickens was that, until now, they had not come across any large animals on the islands they had previously visited. Therefore, they had no reason to suspect that the next port of call (which happened to be New Zealand) would be any different. As it happened, New Zealand already had a large population of giant flightless birds known as *moas*, as well as a unique selection of *other* wildlife.

The moas were probably early descendants of the dinosaurs, some of which grew to a height of 4 metres (13 feet). Other species only grew to 1 metre (about 39 inches). They had feathers, like birds, but unlike ostriches they lacked even the most rudimentary of wings. They had massive, though relatively short, legs. It is interesting to note that in June 1998 the fossil remains of a dinosaur, which had *feathers*, was discovered. So it is quite possible that the moas were the last remaining link between dinosaurs and birds—and Mankind's destructive nature has destroyed them! The *Maoris*, as the settlers became known, began to slaughter these birds, not only for their *flesh*, but also for their *skin* and *feathers*, which they used for clothing and decoration. The bones were used to make weapons and implements. Even the *eggshells* of the moas were used to make drinking vessels and other containers.

To add to the problem, the Maoris then began to clear the forests, which, at the time, covered most of the two islands. As the rape of the forests took place by cutting and burning, so the natural browsing and breeding grounds of the moas began to disappear to make way for human settlements. The Maoris also brought *dogs* with them. These, too, would hunt and kill these unique creatures. On top of all this, uninvited stowaways in the form of rats had boarded the Polynesian ships in search of the inevitable scraps of food on board. They too, had migrated to New Zealand with the human voyagers. The rats bred and thrived in their new home and they found the eggs and chicks of the moas very appetizing! By the time Captain James Cook first visited the islands in 1769 AD, all the true moas were extinct. Mankind had managed to eradicate them all in just 400 years. The only related species left now is the smaller and more agile *kiwi*. It is a sad fact that of the 300 species of birds believed to have lived on the islands before the arrival of the Polynesians, forty-five of them have become totally extinct and many more are severely threatened.

The arrival of the Europeans in the eighteenth century caused even *more* mass destruction. Within *their* vessels *another* species of rat had stowed away. They created further havoc with the local wildlife, not only because of their voracious appetite, but also because of the *diseases* they brought with them.

The Europeans themselves cut down even *more* forests, turning it into pastureland for their sheep. Nowadays, there are more sheep in New Zealand than any other mammal—including Mankind himself! There are now about 55 million sheep in New Zealand and only 3.5 million people. Eighty-three percent of the population are of European

New Zealand Sheep

27

descent, whereas only nine percent is of Maori descent, which goes to show how the Europeans took over. The Europeans didn't care much for the local flora and fauna. They felt more 'at home' with animals they could identify with. The result was that they introduced mallards, blackbirds, rooks, skylarks, starlings, goldfinches and chaffinches from the UK, and parrots, kookaburras and black swans from Australia. In order to continue the European sport of angling, they also introduced *trout* into the rivers and streams. Blood sports were taken care of by the introduction of deer into what forests they had left untouched. They also introduced European flowers and fruit, as well as European crops, with limited success.

The rats and mice, which had travelled with man in his ships, also began to cause problems for *Man* as well as for the environment. They invaded his home and ate his grain and, in an effort to control the problem *weasels* were introduced. This in itself caused further problems for the native wildlife. As a result more indigenous creatures were brought to the very edge of extinction. *Cats* were brought in as pets, and to help control the rodent problem. Many of these abandoned the human towns and villages and became feral. This caused *further* problems for the wildlife. *One* flightless bird, the *takahe,* was *already* close to extinction at the hands of the Polynesians, before the Europeans arrived. Feral cats and weasels put their threatened existence into dire peril. In 1900, the takahe was officially declared extinct. Happily, Man's greedy actions do not reign supreme. In 1948 a small colony of the birds were rediscovered in a remote valley on South Island. It is believed that a colony of some two hundred birds exist there today. Rightfully, the New Zealand authorities now rigorously protect them.

The *kakapo,* a flightless parrot, was *also* hunted relentlessly by the cats and weasels, whilst the deer, which had been introduced specifically for hunting purposes, fed upon the leaves and berries which made up the staple diet of the kakapo. These birds *also* faced extinction until recently, when a small islet, known as *Little Barrier,* was finally cleared of the feral cats. The few remaining kakapo from

Australian parrot

South Island have now been collected together and reintroduced to the islet. Here, hopefully, they will breed and thrive once more.

Other species have not been so fortunate. The *hia,* a species of wattle bird and a good flier, became extinct in the 1900s. Another of the same family, the *saddleback,* was once common across the mainland and islands—it now exists only in very small numbers on an offshore island. It may already be too late to save them. A *third* bird, known as the *kokaka,* now only exists in small numbers on North Island. The large flightless grasshoppers of New Zealand,

Sea life under threat

29

as *wetas,* are *also* becoming increasingly rare. This was directly due to the introduction by Man of trout into the rivers. The trout found the wetas decidedly to their taste. The *tuatara*, a large lizard-like creature, which is more closely related to the dinosaurs than *other* lizards, is now only found in very small numbers on the offshore islands. Before the arrival of Mankind, this survivor of the Mesozoic Age had existed in peace and harmony with its environment for 150 million years. Now its very existence is at peril.

The trout, which, as I have said, had been introduced by the Europeans, have managed to demolish many of the thirty or more species of local fish that once inhabited the streams and rivers of New Zealand. It is a sad fact that many unique species of animal, bird and fish have, or are about to, become totally extinct from 'This Garden Earth' due directly to Man's intervention. It is *also* a fact that Mankind has wiped out whole tribes of his *own species*—and all in the name of 'progress'...

Chapter Four:
When man destroys his own...

The Aborigines of Australia

The native peoples of Australia have caused much discussion amongst scientists. Some argue that they originated as Asian migrants from prehistoric times. Others consider them as purely endemic and a surviving remnant of Neanderthal Man. Generally though, they are regarded as a unique race of Mankind, being classified on their own as *Australoid*.

Either way, they had lived a very primitive life in the stone-age traditions for many thousands of years, until Captain James Cook landed there in 1771. Many of them never wore clothes at all and lived off the natural resources of the land. They never invented the bow and arrow, but were (and still are) extremely proficient with the boomerang and waddy (war club) both of which are used for hunting purposes. The Australian aborigines are remarkably resilient. As well as eating kangaroo and wallaby meat they also consume native plants and roots, and even insects and insect grubs, which they find under the bark of trees.

Fortunately for the natives, the outback (wild inner part) of Australia proved to be too hostile an environment for most Europeans, who settled mainly around the coastal areas. Even so, the arrival of white men on the smallest continent had far-reaching effects upon the natives. At the time of the first white settlements in Australia in 1788 it is estimated that the aborigine population was around 300,000. By the 1970s it had depleted by almost half, to about 160,000. This was due to the native's lack of resistance to the diseases brought over by the white settlers, the disruption of their way of life and the Government's total disregard for the aborigines in the early days.

As I have already said, however, the Australian aborigines are a very hardy race and by 1991 their population had greatly increased to an estimated 257,000. Even so, the white (mainly British) population has increased so much, that nowadays aborigines now account for only 1.5 per cent of the entire population. The Australian aborigines were comparatively lucky, largely due to the hostile environment of the outback, where European migrants rarely ventured. On the neighbouring island of *Tasmania* however, the natives were *not* so fortunate.

TASMANIAN ABORIGINES - THE LAST EARLY STONE-AGE PEOPLE

When the Dutch navigator, Abel Tasman, discovered the island south-west of the Australian mainland, he found it to be a wildly beautiful spot, with high rough hills and a rugged coastline. The island, which is about 40 miles across, was, in his own words, inhabited by 'strange black people'. There was very little on the island to attract settlers at first, though a few brave souls took the chance.

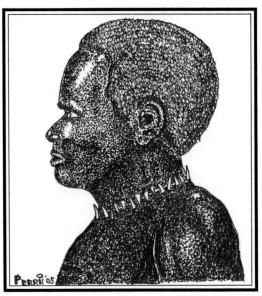

The last native Tasmanian

Then in 1803 Great Britain decided to use it as a penal colony. They sent out 400 convicts. These early colonists called it 'the back of beyond'. Officially, however, it was, at the time, called *Van Dieman's Island*, after Tasman's patron. Van Dieman was the Governor of the Netherlands' West Indies. The convicts were forced to work as slaves for the few free settlers who had taken their chances there. This obviously caused great resentment amongst the convicts and many of them escaped into the wilderness. Out in the wild countryside they teamed up into gangs, returning to kill their previous masters. In 1893 the import of convicts ceased and the government granted the island a representative government. It was renamed Tasmania after its original discoverer.

The *aborigines* of Tasmania, Tasman's 'strange black people', were extremely primitive. Indeed, they had not even reached the *Neolithic,* or 'polished' Stone Age and had barely entered the *Palaeolithic,* or 'crude' Stone Age. They were a simple, peaceful people, quite content in their ancient Stone Age existence. They were totally unaware that the rest of the world had 'progressed' (and I use the term loosely!), leaving them behind evolution-wise by some 500,000 years.

Like much of the Tasmanian wildlife these aborigines were quite unique. Because of this they were hunted down and slaughtered mercilessly by the white settlers and escaped convicts alike for no other reason than that they were 'different'. The very last Tasmanian aborigine died in exile in 1876 and the race became totally extinct—only 73 years after the first white settlers arrived. 'Civilised' man had succeeded in wiping out a whole nation of his own kind. We could have learned *so much* from these people about our *own* origins. Were they the last race of *Neanderthals* to exist on 'This Garden Earth'? We'll never know!

Two *other* species are currently under threat in Tasmania and both are unique to the island. The *Tasmanian devil,* a small bear-like marsupial, is a fierce carnivore with a huge appetite for poultry. At least it *developed* this appetite after the humans *introduced* the poultry. Before that it lived mostly on carrion, though it *did* occasionally hunt rodents, lizards, wallabies and *other* small animals. Because of this appetite for poultry however, the Tasmanian devil has been hunted to the very edge of extinction.

The other creature unique to this island was the *Tasmanian wolf,* a striped wolf-like marsupial that, like the aborigines, was a final relic of the early Stone Age. It was a contemporary of the *smilodon,* or sabre-tooth. When the white settlers began sheep farming the Tasmanian wolf, quite naturally, began attacking the sheep. The white farmers, seeing the creature as a threat to their livelihood, took to hunting the wolf mercilessly. The very last Tasmanian wolf died in captivity in the 1920s.

Tasmanian wolf

NATIVE AMERICANS - A LESSON IN BALANCED LIVING

It is estimated that the race of people once known through western movies as 'Red Indians', but now known more correctly as Native Americans, were originally descended from nomadic tribes who travelled across a land bridge from Siberia and Alaska during the last Ice Age, 25,000 years ago.

Each tribe settled into different parts of North America and developed their own customs and languages. However, they all shared one common belief, which was strongest amongst the Plains tribes. That belief was that human beings are intimately related, not only to *other* living creatures such as animals birds and fish, but *also* to the great mountains and humble stones and, indeed, to The Earth *itself*. They believed that the land they had discovered was a gift from the Creator, or 'Great Spirit'. It was this 'Great Spirit' who actually *owned* the land and the human beings *themselves* were merely the *caretakers* of that land, sharing it with the *other* creations of the 'Great Spirit'. Upon this profound philosophy lay the Native American's economy and their very way of life.

Originally there were several hundred different tribes with names such as *The Sioux, The Mohicans, The Blackfoot, The Iroquois* and *The*

Algonquin. The natives of the eastern wooded area on both sides of the Great Lakes, from The Mississippi River to The Atlantic Ocean, all lived in the great forests, which *covered* this area in bygone days. These tribes carried out some farming techniques, though the menfolk hunted for food, clothing and *other* basic essentials.

The womenfolk, or *squaws,* did most of the work, apart from hunting. It was these womenfolk who became the first farmers in North America. They planted a variety of vegetable marrow known as squashes, wild rice, maize and beans, from which they made the traditional Native American dish, *Succotash.* It was the squaws too, who prepared the skins of animals brought home by the menfolk, or *braves.* They would then proceed to sew them together as clothing for the whole family. They cooked the meat on sharp sticks held over the fire. The hides of the animals were *also* used for covering the tents, or *wigwams.* When the tribe decided to move on and make camp elsewhere it was the squaws who dismantled the camp, carried the burdens and set up again on a new site. They would then light the campfire. As well as being responsible for all these duties they *also* cared for the children, or *papooses,* the youngest of which were carried on the backs of the mothers or hung in a cradle from the branch of a tree, whilst the squaws went about their work.

The reason why these people moved on was a part of their belief. They believed that they should never totally exhaust one area of its resources, so they would move on in order for the land to recover. Something we could well do to learn in *our* society!

Although the squaws did all the work, they were certainly not mere drudges for the braves, nor even for the *Chief* of the tribe. The womenfolk had a distinct say in the policy-making of the tribe. Amongst *The Iroquois* in particular, the braves would not even go on the *warpath* without the consent of the squaws! If a brave disgraced his family in any way, whether it be fighting without permission, or not bringing enough meat home for his family, he would be ordered out of the wigwam or tepee for the night—to sleep alone! If, on the other hand, he had proved himself a great *brave*, the lucky man would not only receive sexual favours from his *own squaw*, but was *also* given a choice of any of her *sisters*! By and large, these Native Americans had established themselves a near-perfect paradise.

The *Eastern tribes* lived during the winter months in long wooden, or bark-built, shacks with a passage down the middle. A stockade would be built around the whole village, merely to protect the inhabitants from predators. They only lived in the *wigwams* in the *summer* months, allowing the shacks to become clear of smoke, which had built up during the *winter* months. The *Plains tribes* however, did not *believe* in barricading themselves in and they lived in their *Tepees* all the time, *whatever* the season. The *Eastern tribes* only joined them when the white settlers forced them out of their villages.

Of all the tribes of North America, the Plains people lived closest to nature as dictated by the teachings of 'The Great Spirit'. They built their entire existence and economy around the *bison* (inaccurately called *buffalo* by early white settlers). When white men first set eyes upon the vast herds of bison he could hardly believe what he was seeing, for it is estimated that there were around 60,000 animals roaming the North American plains at that time. With bows and arrows the Plains people hunted the bison. They ate the flesh, used the hides for clothing, tent coverings and bags, the horns were carved and used for drinking and other vessels and the bones were made into tools, hunting weapons and other implements. Using the sinews and fur they could make ropes and strings for the bows. Nothing was wasted. In today's terminology, they had achieved the perfect ecologically friendly economy.

Not surprising therefore, that the Plains tribes worshipped the bison. The medicine men even wore bison heads as part of their costume, for they believed the animals *themselves* had their own Great Spirit—the Great White Bison. Because of this perfect economy the Plains tribes only killed animals when their needs demanded it. They knew instinctively that they depended upon these great animals for their very existence. To kill indiscriminately would put their *own* livelihood at risk.

White men however, when they first landed upon the shores of the 'New World' in 1492, thought that the 'strange-looking people with bronze, or copper-coloured skins and lank black hair' were 'savage innocents without culture and without any idea of an economy'. It didn't occur to them that these people had a far better culture and economy than their European invaders could ever *dream* of. This was because, unlike the Europeans, their whole lifestyle was *not* based upon greed and personal possession!

IF YOU CAN'T *BRIBE* 'EM, *KILL* 'EM!

In his letter to the King of Spain, *Christopher Columbus* called the natives of North America '*Indios*', because he mistakenly thought that he had reached India. This error has perpetuated through the ages, hence the name '*American Indians*', or '*Redskins*'. The latter is yet *another* misnomer, for there is far less red colouring in the faces of Native Americans than there is in the pink cheeks of '*white*' people! The 'white' Europeans in turn took an instant dislike to the 'red' Indians. The truth was that the natives posed a threat to their plans to colonise the country.

The Europeans simply could not understand the native's philosophy of being 'caretakers' of the land.

The *Piquat tribe* were actually offered *money* for the land by the Europeans. The Europeans could not understand it when they were told, through an interpreter, "Our land is more valuable than your money, for it will last forever. We *cannot* sell you this land, for it does not *belong* to us!" This philosophy was totally alien to the white settlers, who had been brought up in a society where money could buy *anything*. The result was that the settlers wiped out the *entire Piquat tribe* by the seventeenth century.

Other tribes were bribed in various different ways. The white man traded iron pots and rifles for the furs that the natives could produce with such apparent ease. As a result, these people were encouraged to kill the bison indiscriminately during the 1830s. At the same time they inherited firearms, which not only encouraged the wholesale slaughter of even *more* bison, but also gave them the means to fight back at the white settlers on their own terms. The settlers soon learned that one way of getting rid of the 'Indians' as they called them, was to destroy the basis of their entire economy—the bison, and the slaughter of these noble creatures intensified.

As he had done in other countries, white man had brought his own stock of domestic cattle and cereal crops. The great herds of bison upon the plains threatened his own selfish way of life. In 1865, the railway was built right across the continent from east to west. This had the effect of cutting the bison population into two halves. It also impeded the bison's natural migration progress. 'Buffalo Bill' Cody was employed by the railway company to kill as many animals as he could to provide meat for the construction gangs. Cody alone killed 4,280 bison in only eighteen months, and yet he has always been regarded by westerners as one of the 'Wild West Heroes'! On top of this, passengers travelling on the trains were encouraged to shoot bison from the moving trains, merely for the 'sport' of it. This was a cheap way, not only of getting rid of the *bison*, but also of bringing the *Plains tribes* to their knees!

Sometimes the tongues were cut out of the dead animals, as, for a while, this was considered a delicacy amongst the rich settlers. Bison-hide robes were also considered the height of fashion for a time and skinners made a lot of money roaming the plains and skinning the corpses. The remainder of the huge carcasses were largely left to the vultures, or to rot where they lay. During the late 1870s two and a half thousand bison were killed annually and by the end of the decade the entire herd south of the railway had been exterminated. 10,000 of the northern herds were slaughtered in 1883 and by the end of the century there were less than a thousand wild bison left in the whole of North America. Fortunately, common sense prevailed in the early 1900s when legislation was passed to protect the animals. Today, there are about 35,000 bison living in the relative safety of the National Parks.

For 25,000 years the native tribes of North America had built their lives around the bison. They were wise enough to kill them only when the need arose. They were a proud people who lived *with* nature, rather than *against* it. For all that time they had led an idyllic life in harmony with nature. They never knew the meaning of personal possession or greed. On the *other* hand the white man had almost succeeded in slaughtering the bison to extinction in only sixty years, merely for his own selfish ends. In those sixty years he had reduced their numbers from over *sixty million* to less than *one thousand*.

Other creatures too, were slaughtered to the point of extinction. During the nineteenth century it is estimated that there were about 100 million pronghorns roaming North America. By 1908 there were only 19,000 of these antelope-like creatures left. Like the bison, they are now a protected species and today their numbers are approaching half a million.

The Native Americans themselves fought a losing battle, not only against the early settlers and the United States Cavalry, but also as a result of the senseless slaughter of the bison herds. They also perished as a result of diseases that the white man had brought with him. The natives had no resistance to such diseases as tuberculosis and measles and so many of them died after coming into contact with 'carriers' amongst the white settlers. *Of the estimated five million Native Americans living in North America in 1890, only about 250,000 now exist, and many of them are not of pure blood.* In only five hundred years the population of immigrants to North America went from zero to 75 million!

The greed of the white man has been responsible for the extinction and decline of thousands of species of animal and plant life, as well as the wholesale slaughter of his own kind. This has not only been through the 'discovery' of 'new' lands, but also through wars between 'civilised' nations.

TWENTIETH CENTURY SLAUGHTER
The scourge of war will be dealt with in a later chapter, but we cannot pass this chapter without a mention of the horrific slaughter,

via gas chambers, by the Nazis on the orders of Adolf Hitler in World War ll. More than *ONE AND A HALF MILLION PEOPLE* alone, mostly *Jews*, were sent, in their truckloads, to the gas chambers of Auschwitz in Poland, by the Nazis. The bodies were then dumped onto huge funeral pyres to be burnt. The total of Jews exterminated in Nazi concentration camps during this time however, was a sickening *SIX MILLION*.

The Cambodian genocide of 1975-1979, in which approximately 1.7 million people lost their lives (21% of the country's population), was one of the worst human tragedies of the 20th Century. As in Nazi Germany and more recently in East Timor, Guatemala, Yugoslavia and Rwanda, the Khmer Rouge regime headed by Pol Pot combined extremist ideology with ethnic animosity and a diabolical disregard for human life to produce repression, misery and murder on a massive scale.

Similar acts of genocide have been practiced by despots such as Saddam Hussein in Iraq, Idi Amin and Robert Mugabe. During the Iran-Iraq War Saddam Hussein and his forces used chemical weapons against Iran. According to official Iranian sources chemical weapons, between 1983 and 1988, killed approximately 5,000 Iranians. In mid-March of 1988 Saddam Hussein and his cousin Ali Hassan alMajid—the infamous 'Chemical Ali'—ordered the dropping of chemical weapons on the town of Halabja in north-eastern Iraq. This killed an estimated 5,000 civilians. Idi Amin is reputed to have slaughtered 255,000 people in Uganda between 1979 and 1987.

From its inception as an independent nation, Zimbabwe has been ruled by only one man—Robert Mugabe—first as prime minister and since 1987 as president. The country's last general election was held in 1996 and Mugabe won his fourth term as president easily. No one dared oppose him then, he had already 'browbeaten, dismissed and intimidated his rivals'. Mugabe set about killing and terrorizing white landowners and promising their land to his supporters. In the process he's provided a glimpse into the horrific dangers of so-called 'reasonable' gun laws, such as gun registration and gun-owner licensing. Nobody knows how many people he has had slaughtered.

It is estimated that, in the 20th Century alone, somewhere between *sixty and one hundred and twenty million people* have been slaughtered in cases of genocide and ethnic cleansing, and it is all due to greed, mistrust and racial and ethnic prejudice. But before we tut-tut piously at the cruelty of these evil regimes it should be remembered that we in the UK and USA aren't squeaky clean either. The Atom Bomb dropped on Hiroshima on 6th August 1945 by the USA was the first time civilians alone had been targeted. It killed 350,000 people. The bomb dropped on Nagasaki on 9th August 1945 killed 270,000. People were horribly maimed, as well as killed, in Vietnam when the USA used Napalm Bombs. Europe has now banned this evil, inhumane weapon, but the Americans were still using it in Iraq in 2005. We must also remember that many civilians were killed in Germany (particularly in Dresden, which was not a military target) when UK and US bombers retaliated over the Blitzkriegs.

Much of the slaughter of wildlife comes from that most obnoxious trait of humankind—*vanity*…

Hiroshima headlines

CHAPTER FIVE:
SLAUGHTER IN THE NAME OF VANITY
AND STATUS

Like the Native Americans, Stone Age Man killed animals for their meat, using their pelts for clothing, bedding and protection from the weather. He had little choice in the matter, for he was poorly adapted physically for survival in the wild. This meant that he had to use his cunning and superior intelligence.

Man is, however, by his very nature, a show-off. He has an inherent urge to prove how strong, clever, or powerful he is, in much the same way as the 'school bully' does! Because of this basic need to 'prove himself' as an individual, Stone Age Man began to use the spoils of his hunting trips not only for *practical purposes*, but also for symbols of his power or individuality.

Unfortunately, despite our advanced technology and our belief that we are somehow 'superior' to the *other* creatures of 'This Garden Earth', this need to 'prove ourselves' is still with many of us *today*. Just look at politicians 'squaring up to each other' in parliament, or on the International stage. They simply have to 'have one over each other'! Let us now go back to Man's origins in order to discover how this unique trait first came about.

Five million years ago, on the plains of Africa, an ape-like creature existed. He migrated northwards across the land and lived alongside such giant creatures as mammoths, mastodons, giant sabre-tooths, ground sloths, cave bears and huge tusked pigs which grew to the size of a modern-day cow. The tusks of these pigs were over a metre in length, whilst the tusks of the largest mammoths (which grew to a height of up to 4.3 metres) measured 3.2 metres in length. Considering all this fierce opposition, it is a wonder that these early humans survived at all!

In fact, it was the ape-like creatures, early Man, who survived, whilst the others became extinct after living upon 'This Garden Earth' for over two million years. Mammoths became extinct only 10,000 years ago and may have been the first creature to be eradicated by humans.

Woolly mammoth

Modern scientists have given this early Man the name *Australopithecus*. The name means 'southern ape'—popularly termed 'ape-man'. These early ape-men were primarily tree-dwellers and as a result of their arboreal existence they had developed hands with opposable thumbs which could grip. This was an evolutionary development which would eventually enable him to fashion tools and weapons.

Some of these 'ape-men' took to hunting on the plains. In order to improve their field and extent of vision they took to standing upright, adding to their general height. They also possessed bifocal vision, which enabled them to judge distances accurately. This way they were able to observe potential prey and potential predators over the top of the long grass of the plains. Eventually, their bodies adapted to this upright position and they began to walk upright for most of the time. Three million years later these 'ape-men' had developed larger brains. This of course meant that their *skulls* had to grow larger too. By this time they were walking upright continuously.

The 'ape-man' was now nearing the appearance of modern Man and scientists have given him the name of *homo erectus*, or 'upright man'. 'Upright man' was capable of fashioning crude tools and weapons from stone. He was also able to communicate with his fellows by means of body language, hand gestures and crude verbal noises. This was the beginning of language. Because of these unique abilities 'upright man' began to breed profusely, spreading to other parts of the world via 'land bridges' that linked many of the continents in those far-off days.

It is quite likely that Mankind lost the fur that covered his body not by gradual evolution, but rather by spontaneous mutation, caused possibly by some radioactive force from outside the planet. A worldwide disaster maybe, linked to solar activity or meteorites falling to earth. It has even been suggested that modern man *himself* came from another planet—a theory which I will deal with in another book. These theories are more logical than the slow evolution theory, as there was nothing to be gained, at this stage, by the loss of bodily hair. Indeed, it proved to be something of a disadvantage! As Mankind travelled into what is now Europe, the climatic conditions changed. Not having the body hair of his predecessors he would have felt decidedly chilly! Necessity is the mother of invention and, being particularly dextrous with his hands, he soon discovered that the skins of animals that he had killed for meat could be used to cover his *own* body and insulate it against the colder climate. Man had discovered *clothing*.

He *also* learned that this covering could be used as camouflage when hunting prey. A man stalking a wild pig, for example, would more likely go unheeded if he were wearing the *skin* of a pig. Not only would he *look* like a pig, he would also carry the *scent* of a pig—

assuming that the skin was reasonably fresh. In the same way, by using the skins of predators such as sabre tooths, he would go unnoticed by the same species and even scare away other, less powerful predators. So not only had Man now discovered *clothing,* he had also discovered *camouflage.* Even today, many uncivilised tribes use animal skins in this way.

As Man's natural curiosity grew, so he began to make more complex clothing, stitching the skins together to make them a better fit. To do this they made crude needles from bone splinters, using animal sinews for thread. They also began fishing with harpoons, the tips of which were made from multi-barbed bones, as in the vertebrae of birds or the bones of fishes themselves. The tips of *spears,* for the hunting of larger prey, were made from carefully sharpened flint stones. To protect himself further from the elements and dangerous animals he began to live in caves, keeping predators away with fire, which burned constantly, day and night.

As Mankind's language became more complex, he began to express himself in cave paintings. The colours were mixed from minerals and plant pigments, mixed together with a paste made from fine clay and water—terracotta. He had invented not only paint but also dye. As Man's skills grew, so did the complexity of his clothing, paintings and his tools and weapons. These 'intelligent' men evolved about 35,000 years ago. It is quite possible that 'white' man came about as a mutation from the original black. Modern science has given these people the name *homo sapiens,* or 'wise man'. This is what *we* are, but what price 'wisdom'?

Using the skins and other material from dead animals for reasons of status and vanity began innocently enough. After all, this was merely a means to an end, rather than an end unto themselves. It was undoubtedly a tough world out there and Mankind still had to live by nature's prime rule—survival of the fittest. If Stone Age man killed an extra large or fierce beast, whether out of necessity for food or for self-protection, he would keep the teeth, claws or tusks as a trophy and wear them around his neck or waist. Other tribesmen, seeing for themselves the proof of his hunting skills, would come to respect his strength and bravery. These 'great hunters' would often become the leader of the tribe and would have the first choice of females, in much the same way that animals do. A rival tribesman, seeing the proof of his power, would think twice before tackling him. If he was capable of slaughtering a sabre tooth or a giant cave bear single-handedly, what chance would a lesser human being have? *Status symbols* had been discovered and they became common to tribes right across the world.

Some tribes carried the skulls of animals, and even those of defeated *human* enemies, with them in order to prove their prowess as hunters and warriors. From these crude beginnings of wearing bones and teeth around the neck, wrist, waist and even in the earlobes and nostrils came the 'fashion' of wearing jewellery. These things, together with *other* personal possessions led to a way of showing the status of individuals within the tribe.

The original idea of using animal skins for climatic protection and camouflage gave way to its use to denote rank within the tribe and even to identify males from females. When humans ran around *naked* it was *easy*, but with their bodies *covered* the *clothes* had to indicate one sex from the other! In Africa, a chief would wear the skin of a leopard or lion to represent strength and courage. Witch doctors would wear the skins of animals that were regarded as wise or sacred. Young women would wear the skins of elegant, gentle, or beautiful beasts. In Britain and Europe a chief would wear a wolf skin, boar skin, or bear skin, complete with head and teeth. Great hunters would wear the skins of red deer or reindeer, complete with heads and antlers. These customs may well have led to the legends of *Hern the hunter* and the *wolf-man*. The Plains tribes of North America adopted the hides and heads of the bison, which they worshipped as a gift from the Great White Spirit, whilst other tribes used the feathers of predatory birds such as eagles—*another* creature regarded as a great spirit. The more feathers, the higher the status of the warrior or *brave*. The *medicine man* or *Shaman*—the North American counterpart of the

African witch doctor—would wear coyote skins and necklaces made from the teeth of animals.

In *modern* times Mankind has killed animals and birds solely for their skins, feathers, tusks, etc. or merely for 'sport'. As Mankind became more 'civilised', some of his natural instincts became less acute, though much of this depended upon the individual and his place in society. Over the millennia Man has lost much of the acuteness of his senses of smell and hearing, plus the ability to detect the earth's magnetic poles and subtle changes in the environment. Animals and birds *still* rely on these senses to enable them to travel (and in the cases of some birds, circumnavigate the earth) and to detect the imminence of natural disasters. Unfortunately, man has totally lost these abilities through living in a synthetic environment and from relying upon scientific instruments.

The need to procreate however has largely stayed with him. This, together with advances in medical knowledge, has ensured that Mankind has become the most numerous and most widely distributed of all the earth's mammals. Ten thousand years ago there were only about ten million people living on 'This Garden Earth'. Four thousand years ago, with the advancement of civilisation, their numbers began to increase rapidly, reaching a total of three hundred million. In the 1970s there were in excess of *four thousand million* human beings walking the earth. At the beginning of this, the second, millennium there were 6,200 million people living on the earth—that's an incredible *6.2 BILLION* of us!

This seemingly unstoppable advance of the human race threatens the ecological balance of the planet and puts a great strain upon the earth's resources. So great is this threat that nature appears to have introduced 'culling' methods in an attempt to decrease human over-population. This has been in many forms from earthquakes, floods, tornados, tsunamis and volcanic activity, to diseases that are peculiar to the human race and their livestock. We have seen, in recent times the onset of AIDS, BSE, CJD, E-Coli, Scrapie, Legionnaires disease, Ebola, countless *other* new tropical diseases and nanobacteria, which appears to account for *many* peculiarly human diseases. Even Mankind *himself* has subconsciously tried to cull his own population growth with warfare and acts of unsolicited violence, as in the ill-fated Bush/ Blair war in Iraq, which has served to *increase* terrorism rather than *stem* it! This is what I call the 'lemming factor'.

He has also introduced synthetic contraceptives, which, ironically, have been encouraged more since the advent of AIDS. A threat to human survival has also come from our own actions against nature. Pollution has given rise to more cases of impotency and is also causing a decrease in the sperm count of human males. In many human individuals the *destructive* instinct appears to be overtaking the *procreation* instinct, which is common in *other* animals.

Since Mankind gave up his natural life in favour of 'civilisation' he appears to have developed into two distinct categories, the 'aggressors' and the 'pacifists'. Unfortunately, because of their very nature—a desire to control others—the aggressive humans *always* reach the pinnacle of power. It is these individuals who hold in their hands the future of the *rest* of us—and indeed, the future of the *entire planet*…

CHAPTER SIX:
THE WEAPONS OF DESTRUCTION

It is difficult to know exactly when Mankind first discovered that he could kill an animal from a distance by hurling a missile at it. Certainly it began with the throwing of stones and sticks, as many apes, particularly chimpanzees, wave sticks or throw stones to warn off aggressors today.

In Australia some tribes must have discovered that *curved* sticks, thrown at the right angle, would return to the thrower, giving birth to the idea of the boom-erang. The next stage was probably some form of sling made from animal skins, followed by a catapult made from a forked twig across which was stretched animal sinews or strong vines. It seems likely that these slings and catapults were used to propel stones, as many tribes across the world do today.

Sling shot

Next came the spear, made from a long staff of wood tipped with a sharp flint. It wouldn't have been long before someone realised that the spears and catapults could be combined to make the first bow and arrow. This development *must* have happened during the Stone Age, as men with bows and arrows are depicted in many prehistoric cave paintings.

Obviously the invention of the bow and arrow would have greatly increased Mankind's power over other animals, as he could now kill any animal, great or small, swiftly, whilst taking cover himself. This was something no other animal could do. The *short bow,* as it has come to be known, was still used by the Saxons and the Normans at the Battle of Hastings in 1066 AD, though by now the tip of the arrows were made of *metals,* rather than *flint.* This development took place firstly during the *Bronze Age* about 2000 BC, until bronze was replaced by iron during the *Iron Age* around 1200 BC. The bow and arrow spread rapidly throughout the world with a few exceptions, notably in Australasia, where the main hunting weapons were still slings and boomerangs.

The archers of Merrie Englande!

The *longbow* was probably developed by the *Welsh* during the twelfth century and was introduced into England by Edward 1, soon after his Welsh campaign in 1274 AD. The longbow soon became England's standard weapon, both for hunting purposes and for battle. Indeed, every Sunday, during mediaeval times, English village greens were dotted with groups of men practising their archery skills. This practice was actually encouraged by law and all other sport was forbidden on the Sabbath. English archers were rated the best in the world, winning battles at *Crecy, Poitiers* and *Agincourt.* With this formidable weapon, they could also hunt animals more effectively for meat, fur or for 'sport'. It was the use of the longbow that finally wiped out the remaining *bears, wolves, beavers* and *wild boars* from the British countryside, although a few bears *were* retained for a while, for the mediaeval 'sport' of bear-baiting.

In *those* days the wild boar was considered a great delicacy of the English aristocracy and no banquet was complete without a boars head carried into the banqueting hall on a silver salver. Often an apple or some *other* fruit such as a medlar or quince was placed into the boar's mouth as a garnish. Travellers, woodsmen and outlaws also hunted the wild boar as they found the meat both tasty and highly nutritious. As a result the last wild boar in England was killed in 1683. In Europe however, they are still preserved on large estates for the purpose of digging up truffles, and for hunting!

At about the time of the development of the longbow in England the Europeans were developing the *crossbow* or *arbelest*. This was a short, powerful bow mounted upon a stock, which had a groove or barrel cut out to guide the *bolt* or *quarrel*. The bowman would put his foot into a stirrup whilst he braced the cord. This was done mainly by means of a rack or lever, although sometimes a windlass and pulley were used. The cord was held in a catch and released by a trigger. Although quite effective in *hunting* if the bow was ready cocked, it was slow and clumsy for use in *battle*. It was certainly no match for the longbow, which, in the hands of an expert archer, could be loaded, aimed and fired with great accuracy at the rate of *an arrow every ten seconds!* However, the crossbow *did* herald the beginning of *mechanical weaponry*, which could propel missiles at a greater distance and at a greater force.

CHINESE CRACKERS!

Amazingly Chinese alchemists discovered a mixture of *saltpetre*, *charcoal* and *sulphur* in the 11th Century. Today it is known as *gunpowder!* Oddly enough the Chinese themselves never fully realised the potential of gunpowder as a means of destruction. They used it instead for the production of flares and fireworks. It is said that the 13th Century Mongol emperor, *Jenghiz* (*Genghis*) *Khan* first realised it's potential as a destructive explosive whilst being received as a 'guest' of the Chinese emperor. He noticed that, when confined, the powder would cause a great explosion if ignited and that the resulting explosive force was capable of propelling a missile at great speed and force from a tube or barrel. These first crude cannons were used by the Mongols to defeat the *Tartars* and, ironically, the *Kin* dynasty of *China!* Khan finally took Peking in 1214 AD.

It was not until more than one hundred years later, in about 1320, that gunpowder was first manufactured in Europe. In *those* days a cannon simply consisted of a long tube that was closed at one end. The gunpowder was then placed in the bottom of the tube and a stone was pushed down the tube on top of the gunpowder. Near to the closed end of the tube was a small hole, known as the *touch-hole*. A lighted taper was pushed down this to ignite the powder. Naturally the gunpowder exploded, forcing the stone out of the open end. This weapon was certainly quite effective in times of war, but not really any good for hunting! It is interesting to note that at *this* stage Mankind had gone back to throwing *stones!*

By the mid-sixteenth century, when alloys were being produced, it became possible to make lighter, stronger gun barrels. These could be mounted on a set of two wheels and pulled by galloping horses. At about the same time old *stone-shot* was replaced with *cast-iron cannon balls*. These, in turn, were eventually replaced by *hollow* balls, which could be filled with more gunpowder. These hollow missiles were made with long fuses which, when ignited by the explosion of the gunpowder in the barrel of the cannon, would explode upon impact. The first crude *bomb* had arrived!

During the following 300 years gun barrels became stronger. More powerful gunpowder drove the cannonballs over greater distances. Then ballistics experts figured out that a *ball-shaped* missile was pretty ineffective when compared to a *cylinder* that was *flat* at one end and *pointed* at the other—the now-familiar *bullet* shape. Unfortunately, when these bullet-shaped missiles were first tried out they spun eccentrically when they left the smooth-barrelled gun, thus impeding the trajectory. It wasn't until the middle of the 19th Century that somebody came up with the idea of a *grooved* gun barrel and a *cylinder-shaped* shell with a *driving band*. The practice of *rifling* was born.

Don't trifle with the rifle!

Once again though, these large guns were very effective during *battles* but were of little use in *hunting*. In fact the idea of using the cannon principle for firearms or handguns had already occurred in the 15th Century. This consisted of an iron tube, some three feet long, attached to a straight piece of wood known as a *stock*. One end was closed to form the *breech* and a small opening was situated an inch or so *from* the breech, in the barrel. This was known as the *touch- hole*.

Again, gunpowder was poured down the muzzle and a few small stones or metal balls were rammed down into the gunpowder. The gun itself was held by the barrel with the left hand, whilst the stock was firmly tucked under the right armpit. A burning taper or match of cotton cord soaked in saltpetre was then applied to the *touch-hole*, causing the gunpowder to explode and eject missile or missiles. These early handguns seldom had a range of more than one hundred feet and were notoriously inaccurate. Besides this, the gun would often explode in the hand, injuring, or even *killing,* the gunner! So still the archer reigned supreme!

Handguns were used mainly to *frighten* the enemy with the noise and smoke it produced more than anything else, for they weren't much use for actually *killing* anything, apart, perhaps, from the people who were *using* them! Towards the end of the fifteenth century an *improved* handgun, the *arquebus*, was introduced. This had a curved stock with a wide end, butt-shaped, to fit snugly against the gunman's shoulder. However, it was so heavy that the barrel had to be rested upon a forked post stuck into the ground whilst aiming. Soon however, the arquebus was improved by fixing a hammer, which held the taper or lighted match over the touch-hole. This hammer was released by pulling a trigger. This gun was known as a *matchlock*. The matchlock had a very short range, so the *Spaniards* increased the length of the barrel and renamed it the *musket*. The word came from the *French* word '*mousquet*', meaning 'sparrowhawk'. This was because the weapon was first used for the shooting of *birds*. So, at last, an effective *hunting weapon* had been invented!

A much *safer* gun appeared in the middle of the sixteenth century with the invention of the *wheel lock*. This lock consisted of a steel wheel, grooved with a milled edge, like that of a cigarette lighter. This was wound by a key, situated against the tension of the spring. The wound-up wheel was then held by a trigger. When the trigger was pulled the spring unwound, causing the wheel to revolve at a rapid speed, its milled edge rubbing against the flint. This action produced sparks, which ignited the gunpowder. Wheel locks were used mainly in pistols, for they were far too complicated and expensive for general usage. So at this stage, most guns continued to be fired with the aid of a lighted match, until the first *flintlock* was invented in about 1650 AD.

In the flintlock a hammer was used with a piece of flint screwed into the head. When the trigger was pulled the hammer sprung forward, causing the flint to strike a piece of roughened steel mounted over a covered pan, which held the gunpowder. The movement of the trigger uncovered the pan and the striking of the flint upon the steel caused a spark. This ignited the gunpowder, firing the charge of powder in the barrel. Of course the gunpowder still had to be rammed down the barrel of the gun. This weapon had a range of no more than 50 yards and it needed a new flint after about every 20 shots. Even so it remained in general use until about 1840, when the British army replaced the flintlock with the *percussion lock*. It is interesting to note that even in the 19th Century flint was still being used to cause a spark, just as our Stone Age forebears did when they first discovered fire!

OUT OF THE FLINTSTONE AGE!

Alexander Forsyth invented the percussion lock in 1802, and it was first used only in *sporting* guns. It was not adopted for *military* use until forty years later. The cap was based upon the fact that certain explosives, *fulminates*, explode when struck sharply. In the *percussion cap* gun a small piece of pointed metal was mounted perpendicularly onto the breech. Upon this was placed a small copper cap, containing the fulminate. When the trigger was pulled the hammer would fall and explode the cap, sending a jet of flame into the powder. This in turn explodes, driving the bullet out of the barrel. This principle is still used today in *modern* guns.

The only problem now was that the bullets had to be of a large calibre in order to give them the weight necessary to carry them any distance and to strike the target with any force. The result was that the range was still very short and, as they offered tremendous resistance to the wind, they were wildly inaccurate. To *add* to these problems the bore of the barrel was smooth, causing the bullet to roll over and over as it left the barrel. In order to *overcome* this the principle of *rifling* was readopted, by cutting grooves along the inside length of the gun barrel, as had previously been used in cannons. When the rifle was fired the grooves gripped the sides of the bullet as it passed through the barrel. This caused the missile to spin along it's own length, giving it greater range and accuracy.

The first really *efficient* rifle was the *breech loader*, which used cone-shaped bullets to the end of which was fitted a metal case containing the explosive charge. In the base of this gun was a fulminate cap. When this cap was struck by a pin controlled by the trigger the charge exploded, expelling the bullet through the barrel of the rifle. Once this principle was perfected *magazines* of bullets were introduced so that the bullets did not have to be loaded individually. Nowadays, the smooth bore gun is *still* used for sporting purposes, although they are *breech loading* and use *cartridges* containing a number of shots or pellets. These spread out into a spray as they leave the barrel, giving 'sportsmen' more chance of hitting a small, quick-moving target such as a bird or a rabbit. This is tantamount to a Stone Age man throwing a *fistful* of stones at his quarry, rather than a single stone, in the hope that one will hit the target. The difference is that, in *those* days, man *relied* upon hunting for his *survival*. Nowadays, at least in the *industrialised* nations, he *doesn't!* Hunting in *modern* times is merely an outlet for bloodlust and personal indulgence, at the expense of *other* forms of life.

So it was that Mankind, throughout the ages, went about killing animals, not only for food and other essentials, but also for reasons of vanity, status, excitement and greed. The feathered headdresses of the North American Native can now be seen in the form of ostrich, lyrebird and peacock feathers upon the hats of rich ladies. The ancient chief's animal-hide costumes, used originally for camouflage and hunting purposes, can now be seen as expensive fur coats made out of mink, ocelot, leopard, seal and many *other* beautiful creatures. The teeth, tusks and bones displayed by ancient warriors and hunters as a sign of their skills, can now be observed in the ivory and bone ornaments adorning the homes of the wealthy.

The principal, despite our so-called 'sophistication', remains much the same, though the motives have changed. Ancient Mankind wore skins and jewellery, displaying teeth and tusks in order to show other tribesmen that he was strong and powerful. In *modern* times, expensive fur coats, hats, jewellery and ornaments show *others* in society that the wearer or owner is *also* powerful, though in a different way. The power of modern man lays in how much money he has. The rarer the furs, feathers, jewellery or ornaments, the more expensive they become—and the greater it's effect upon the status of the owner. The main difference between the motives is that the ancient warrior/ hunter would wear his furs, feathers and 'jewellery' and display his 'possessions' to show others how strong or cunning he was. It showed that he could overpower great beasts and these artefacts were proof of his skills. In the *modern* world however, strength and cunning do not come into it! *Monetary* wealth is what matters today.

The rich people who wear fur and feathers and who display ivory and fine ornaments in their homes no longer have to kill the animals themselves. They pay *others* to do it *for* them! They also pay others to carve ornaments, sew and put items of clothing together for them. The original driving force is no longer *bravery and cunning*, or even *skill*. It is purely born out of *vanity* and *greed*. No longer is it a case of *needing* something, it is now a case of *wanting* something for purely selfish reasons.

Huntsmen don't chase and kill foxes or deer out of *necessity* any more, *whatever* they may wish us to believe. They are not the pests some would like us to believe and they are certainly not *edible!* Foxes have as much right to roam this earth and hunt for food as any *other* creature, as do *deer*. It is no longer necessary to kill deer for their *meat*, it can be brought from the butchers, who get it from the farm and slaughterhouses. This killing is done purely for the fun and excitement of it all, which puts the huntsmen on a much lower evolutionary scale than their Stone Age forefathers. It is this vanity and greed that has brought about the wholesale slaughter of many of the earth's animals, birds, fish, reptiles and plants and led to the *chainsaw massacre...*

Fallow deer

CHAPTER SEVEN:
THE CHAINSAW MASSACRE

With the development of more sophisticated weapons Mankind was capable of slaughtering more and more wild animals, as well as more of his own kind. Anything which had attractive fur, like the leopard, cheetah, ocelot, seal, fox and many more, were shot or trapped indiscriminately to make coats for wealthy ladies. These 'socialites' believed that the grace of the unfortunate animal would somehow be transferred to *them*, via the coat or wrap made from its fur. Actually, there was little chance of that! An animal's markings, however beautiful they may appear to *us*, have been developed over the millennia for specific purposes. They may act as camouflage against would-be predators or for the attraction of a mate. Did these 'ladies' believe the coat could do the same for *them*? In *this* respect these 'upper-crust' people were no more civilised than the tribesmen of long ago, who believed that a particular power would be transferred to *them*, simply by wearing the *fur* of an animal.

Smaller animals, such as *mink*, were reared in special farms especially for the making of coats and stoles. These little creatures were killed in their *hundreds*, simply to make *one* mink coat. Many of the American minks, imported into Europe especially for the fur trade in the twentieth century, escaped, forming colonies across Europe, including Britain. They wreaked havoc with the natural wildlife.

In Europe and Britain fox and wolf pelts were highly prized to provide fur wraps for the 'ladies about town'. In the 1920s and 1930s it was fashionable for these 'ladies' to wear a *whole fox pelt*, complete with head and tail, around the neck. The 'Masters of the Hounds' must have been on to a nice little earner selling these pelts to the fur trade! The *wolverine* too, once common throughout North America, Europe and Asia, was a fashionable fur, with the result that this animal came very close to total extinction, despite the fact that they were adept at robbing traps set for other animals.

Other skins, such as those of the *bear*, *tiger* and *jaguar* were used to make expensive rugs for expensive households, whilst *racoons* were slaughtered to provide hats for pioneers to the 'New World'. These, like the one worn by Davy Crockett, were meant to give visitors the impression that the men of the household were 'brave hunters', especially if the walls of the household were adorned with the complete, stuffed heads of animals such as *deer* and *elk*. 'Fashionable' homes in Britain often displayed the mounted heads of *lions*, *tigers* and other 'big game', providing the big game hunters of yesteryear with a healthy income.

Smaller animals such as *mongoose*, *badgers*, *foxes* and even *fish* were killed, stuffed and displayed in glass cases, along with wall-mounted display cabinets containing preserved *moths* and *butterflies*, stuck to the board with a pin. Not the *best* way to preserve wildlife, I think you may agree! The *mongoose* display was popular with tourists and soldiers serving in Asia during the Second World War, who would bring them back as souvenirs. Often they would be mounted with a stuffed poisonous snake, such as a *cobra*, and arranged in such a manner that the mongoose appeared to be *attacking* the snake.

Crocodiles and *alligators* gave up their skins, and their lives, to provide soldiers with 'gaiters' and rich civilians with expensive shoes, handbags and wallets. *Elephants* were slaughtered by the thousand, merely to provide the ivory trade with ornate carvings and piano keys. The massive carcasses were left where they lay to rot and decay, in the same manner that the bison had been in North America. Hunting elephants for ivory is now illegal, but poachers still make a huge profit in this hideous trade on the black market.

As Mankind's *weapons* became an increasingly effective means of slaughtering man and beast alike, so the *tools* he developed became more destructive to *plant life* and the whole of 'This Garden Earth's' ecological balance. Possibly the most *destructive* of these tools has been the *chainsaw*. Of course, Mankind has been chopping down trees and clearing woodland, forest and jungle since the invention of the stone axe at least 12,000 years ago. Since then he has destroyed trees, plus the life living in *them,* to make way for villages, towns, cities and then motorways, with little or no regard for the catastrophic effects his actions have on wildlife. The trees themselves have been used for the production of paper, furniture, ships and boats, for houses and moulds for the making of bricks and concrete blocks. The timber trade has been a thriving industry for centuries. Britain even proudly boasted that their ships were made from 'hearts of oak'.

What Mankind did not *realise* in those days was that trees play an essential role in the ecological balance of the entire planet. Not only do they provide oxygen for *all* animal life and absorb carbon dioxide to prevent the planet from *overheating,* they also hold the *soil* together and provide *homes* and *food* for countless millions of animals, birds, insects and certain other plants, such as ivy, moss and fungi. Trees even play an important role in the earth's complex *weather systems*!

Alas! Many of the great forests of Europe, Asia and the Americas have been destroyed in the name of 'progress'. All that is left now of any great consequence are the earth's tropical rainforests and already, during the twentieth century, almost two-thirds of them have been destroyed. This constitutes some 30 million species of plant and animal life that has been lost forever. Moreover, much of this has occurred in the latter half of the twentieth century!

The last great rainforest in Sarawak, Malaysia, is home to 400,000 forest people, the *Penon,* as well as countless millions of plants, animals, birds and *other* creatures. This is now coming under grave threat due to the thoughtless actions of modern man. By far the largest consumer of hardwood from the Sarawak rainforest is *Japan.* This country uses *one third* of the total world output and a massive *ninety per cent* of all the trees that are felled in the whole of Malaysia. The forest people of Malaysia, *the Penon,* are one of only a *handful* of nomadic hunting people still left on the earth. Like the North American Natives, of which we spoke in chapter four, the

Penon do not want any money for the land and they are vehemently opposed to any development which would totally destroy their existence. Quite understandably so! All these people really want is to be left alone with the trees which have sustained them for as long as any of them can remember. Now, however, their very lives are threatened, together with those of billions of insects, birds, animals, fish and plants, thanks to 'civilised' Man.

In December 2005 it was announced that a new species of carnivore—a cat-like animal with dark red fur and a bushy tail—had twice been photographed at night with camera-traps laid in the dense forests of Borneo. This was the first new species of animal found in the region for over one hundred years and scientists were terribly excited. Unfortunately, the discovery was announced just as plans were unveiled by the Indonesian Government to develop the World's largest Palm Oil Plantation, covering an area of 1.8 millions hectares of the rainforest. That is equivalent to half the area covered by The Netherlands! The new species, which obviously exists in extremely small numbers, will be rendered extinct by this development, together with hundreds of other species of plant and animal life. We never learn, do we?

Cat-like mammal of Borneo

If you were to stand in Tokyo, Japan, and look across the harbour, you would see that for half a mile ahead, and for the same distance either side, the water is a solid mass of floating logs. They all come from Malaysia! The trees that once stood tall and grand, providing homes for billions of living creatures and supplying food and shelter for the forest dwellers, now lay dead in a featureless landscape, enveloped by choking smog, which is the Tokyo atmosphere. The rivers of Sarawak run shallow with silt from the felling of these magnificent trees. This of course, kills the fish and all the *other* life in the water. Apart from the thoughtless waste of natures' infinite beauty, this also deprives the Penon of one of their basic foods—fish.

Plants and animals, which have not even been identified, are becoming extinct, for here there are species that survive nowhere else on earth. Another part of the Penon's staple diet comes from the wild game and sago palms, but these are fast being destroyed as the chainsaw massacre continues relentlessly. The forest dwellers have to retreat further and further into their dwindling forest home, trying to hang on to the threads of their existence. This, however, is of little use, for the chainsaws are never far behind, destroying everything in their path.

Woodland clearance - Scotland

Many of the younger forest dwellers have given up the struggle for survival in the forest and have settled in towns, where they are exploited for ridiculously low wages and have to pay for the very items which were once given to them by nature. Like the North American Natives, the Tasmanian and Australian Aborigines and many *other* previously isolated races, they fall foul of diseases that they had never before been in contact with.

In 1990 the leader of the Penon, *Juwi Leban*, estimated that if the logging continued at the present rate, the entire forest would have been wiped out in four years. Many of his people took to sitting down in front of the encroaching bulldozers. Unfortunately, they were up against corporate greed, modern politics and business interests, and the chainsaw massacre continued. Also in 1990 Japan gave £11 million in 'aid' to Malaysia. Much of this was spent on the building of logging roads! The problem is that the politicians of Sarawak have financial interests in most of the logging companies, so they are hardly likely to bother about the environment! As many Penons try to hinder the work of these companies, in order to protect their own lifestyles, they end up in jail for obstruction. They are actually penalised for trying to protect their own homeland and natural way of life!

It is the same the world over. Whether it be in Malaysia or Britain, the people who try to protect the earth by protesting at the 'official vandals', by risking their lives in order to stop the massacre, society labels 'criminals'. They are consequently arrested. In a perfect world it would be the *protesters* who would be hailed as the heroes, for trying to protect the Earth for our future generations. The civil engineers should be the ones who are thrown in jail—for crimes against the planet!

This however, is one of the symptoms of our sick society. Common sense no longer prevails. Every time politics and the economy are set higher up the agenda, whilst ecology and the environment take a back seat. They don't appear to grasp the simple fact that if we don't change our ways there won't be an earth to fight over *at all!*

But back to Malaysia. Much of the wood taken from the forest is used to build Japanese houses and office blocks. So here we have a prime example of a 'sophisticated' society bleeding a simple society dry for no less reason than that of pure greed. The saddest part of all is that the wood is not even put to permanent use! It is turned into plywood panels to make mouldings for concrete. Once the concrete structures are cast, the wood is destroyed! *What a waste of nature's precious wealth!* Ironically, much of Japan *itself* is dense in forestland between the mountains, though nowhere near as vast as that in Malaysia. It has proved far too expensive for the Japanese to exploit their *own* trees however. Buying timber from poor Asian countries is much cheaper. Once again it is a case of never minding the *ecology—* think of the *economy!*

Softwood is even imported by the Japanese to make the *two-and-a-half billion chopsticks* they use and throw away every year! That works out at about 170 pairs for every person in Japan. Countries all across the globe have protested at Japan's attitude and apparent disregard for the environment, but of course, politicians are nervous about upsetting them *too* much as they play a big part in world economy with goods such as cars and electrical equipment! Even so the European parliament has demanded an end to logging in an indigenous land. In the 1990s more than one thousand European cities banned the use of rainforest timbers, yet *still* Japan continues to increase its imports. Japan's imports increased in 1990 by 27 per cent from *Sarawak*, by 59 per cent from the *Philippines* and by a *full one hundred per cent* from *Vietnam!* At the same time the Japanese government announced plans to build *seven million* new houses, all from timbers felled in the rainforests.

For nine months, from July 1997 to April 1998, forest fires raged in Borneo destroying much of the rainforests. Thousands of rare trees were destroyed, as were many animals. Thousands of Orang-utans perished, not only through the fire *itself,* but also because many forest dwellers, unable to eat their *usual* diet, had no choice but to kill them for food. Several factors caused this environmental catastrophe.

Global warming and the effects of *El Nino* meant that the rainy season was delayed. On top of this, loggers were burning timber and farmers burned areas to clear the ground. These factors caused the fires to get totally out of control. Mind you, it is all very well Europeans pointing an indignant finger at the Japanese and other 'foreigners', *all* 'civilised' countries, *particularly* the Europeans, have, at one time or another, exploited forests and jungles in the same way. As we have seen from previous chapters of this book and in *This Garden Earth*.

In Britain we still dig up our own countryside and clear woodland and forests to create towns and motorways, as do all *other* developed and developing countries. In the late 1990s there was great consternation amongst locals and conservationists regarding the British governments' plans to build five million new homes across the English countryside. They planned to build these on one thousand square miles of greenbelt land. There were unprecedented protests from people living in places such as Stevenage, Hertfordshire (my home town), where they intended to build 10,000 of these homes on green belt land, Milcheldever Hants, where 8,000 were planned, Newcastle-upon-Tyne, where 2,500 houses plus a business park were to be built and Broadlyst and South Hamps, Devon, where it was planned to build 3,000 around each town. The rest were planned for Chester, Lincoln and the Severn vale, Gloucester, between Chelmsford and Colchester in Essex and around Bradford in West Yorkshire. At the time of writing, and despite protests, not only from environmentalists but also from members of the general public, the government is still determined to go ahead with this continuation of the chainsaw massacre.

Throughout the world governments continue to ride roughshod over public opinion and fail to recognise the damage we are doing to the very future of this planet and all the life upon it. Moreover, the police and military are trained to see any protesters as the 'enemy', whatever their motives. Even so, governments cannot ignore public opinion indefinitely, for it is that public who keeps the politicians where they are. There is no such thing as an *'innocent bystander'* when it comes to matters of the natural environment, for if you stand by and say nothing you are as guilty as the perpetrators themselves.

One thing that people do not seem to take into account when speaking about Mankind's thoughtless interference with nature is *light pollution*! In Britain numbers of glow-worms are on the decline and the main reasons are probably these:

- *Decline or changes in habitat* When you go to the sites in the historical county-by-county records you find that many have now been built on or have been 'improved' in some way (e.g. an open space has now been 'parkified' by the removal of weeds.

- *Use of pesticides and herbicides* This is bound to have an effect on the prey of glow-worms and on the insects themselves.

- *Artificial lighting* This has increased in extent enormously since the 1960s and few landscapes are now free from light pollution. Even in country areas householders' 'security' lights blaze across wide areas. There is no doubt that male glow-worms are attracted to artificial lighting of any colour and this must distract them from finding females. Of course, without a detailed long-term site survey with accurate and consistent before-and-after results there is no firm evidence that this does cause a decline. However, most glow-worm sites are in dark areas and this suggests that lights do cause a decline.

- *Changes in land use* Much of what was open downland (such as on the Chilterns and South Downs) is now no longer grazed by sheep, allowing them to become increasingly overgrown. Glow-worms prefer open areas to dense undergrowth. The increasing amount of set-aside land may be a positive change in the short term if there are glow-worms nearby to colonise the area. Recently we have become concerned that sheep grazing might not be as beneficial as we thought. In the past both sheep and rabbits would keep the grass short, but rabbits are now often shot, leaving it all to the sheep. Sheep's urine may be bad for snails, removing the glow-worms' food supply. We need to find sites where there are known changes in management and reliable counts of glow-worm numbers to see if there is anything in this.

Like the chainsaw, *other* tools and machinery have played havoc with the natural environment. These include such tools as *mining and drilling* equipment. This is yet *another* case of Mankind putting his own interests above anything else, without a single thought for the ultimate consequences ...

CHAPTER EIGHT:
RAPE AND PILLAGE!

What are popularly called 'the Earth's resources' were laid down by the forces of nature millions of years ago. Yet Mankind, in his greed and selfishness, has plundered and wasted them within just a few centuries. Indeed, we have used up *one third* of the Earth's natural resources within the past *25 years*! We should remember that they are *the Earth's* resources—not *Mankind's!*

FOR PEAT'S SAKE!

Peatland once covered millions of acres throughout the British Isles, Russia, Germany, Denmark, Scandinavia, North America and other countries within The Earth's temperate zone. Peat is an inert form of humus, formed over millions of years by vegetation dying and rotting in watery places. If left where it lay further natural conditions over thousands of years would turn this into coal. A peat bog is soft and spongy. It absorbs water easily, presenting ideal conditions for the growth of reeds, rushes, mosses, and other bog plants such as the moisture-loving primulas, monkey musk, asphodel and the insectivorous plants such as sundews, pitcher-plants, butterworts and the Venus

Pitcher plant

fly trap. The peat itself, in parts goes down to a depth of forty feet.

For centuries Mankind has dug out this peat with child-like abandon for his own use. This is because peat burns very slowly when dried, although it also produces a lot of smoke. In Ireland it is still used as a substitute for coal, at a great cost to the natural environment. Over the past forty years, in Britain alone, man has destroyed more than half of our wetlands. Not only has this put many of our native moisture-loving plants in great peril, it has also drastically reduced our natural populations of frogs, newts and dragonflies, some species of which are now close to extinction.

Peat bogs are always situated upon watertight foundations, where the decay of bog plants and fallen vegetation continues relentlessly— *if* left to nature. As the plants living on the surface continue to grow, the decomposing remains of previous generations of plant beneath the surface become thicker and more compressed. Firstly the site may be a pond. As the decomposing material builds up it then becomes a mire, then a peat bog and then, if left to nature, it becomes a moor.

There are, in fact, several different *types* of peat, according to the plants and trees that predominated the site at the beginning of its formation. From time to time the types of plants may have changed, quite naturally locally, over the millennia. This is apparent in the colour and substance of the various layers that are only revealed when the peat is dug out. Upon examination of the peat it will be found to contain fragments of plants, insects and tree remains, sometimes perfectly preserved. Even animal and *human* remains have been found in peat.

Originally peat was dug out of the ground in the form of wet slabs by means of long-handled spades, especially shaped for the job. Nowadays however, the big peat producers use sophisticated machinery. There is likely to be as much as eighty per cent water in these slabs. These are traditionally set up to dry in the sun and wind. After this process the slabs may still contain up to twenty per cent moisture, but they are still *burnable* in this condition. They can now be compressed into *briquettes,* which are easier to handle. After they have been dried out even further by mechanical means the peat can even be used to produce gas for cars. Peat tar and ammonia liquor, dyes and plastics can *all* be extracted from this and *still* the treated peat can be used for burning.

Many people, in various parts of the world, are still allowed, by their governments, to cut their own local peat for free, although more and more sites are now being taken over by the huge combines. In the *commercial* peat industry, mechanical diggers are used. Light railway tracks are laid down so that the slabs can be moved quickly and efficiently with the minimum amount of labour involved. Even before digging *begins,* drainage channels are dug around the sites in order to make the cutting easier. This, of course, is *disastrous* for the wildlife—though *good* for profits!

The commonest use for peat *nowadays* however, especially in Britain, Europe and the USA is for *horticultural* purposes. The peat, usually bought by gardeners in bales or plastic bags, is quite simply dug into the garden to improve the condition of the soil. It is also used extensively in *potting composts* and even as litter in *stables*. Unfortunately, the gardeners' gain is nature's loss. The gain for the gardener is strictly *short term*, for the peat very quickly rots away in dry soils. Recently, however, there have been efforts to encourage gardeners to use *peat-free* composts—though *still* the peat industry continues! The loss to the planet however, is extremely *long-term*, for even if the holes left by the peat-diggers are filled up with waste vegetation (man's pathetic attempt to balance the scales), it will take *millions of years* for nature to turn it into peat again. Even *that* is assuming the site had not been *pre-drained* and that Mankind allows nature to take its course, which by past records is *extremely unlikely*!

Evidence of the existence of peat bogs has been found in Cromer, Norfolk. A great number of tree stumps, complete with roots, were found there. These are what scientists call *forest beds*. Of the *thirty* species of large land animals found there, as fossilised remains, *only six exist anywhere in the world today*. The rest are now totally *extinct*.

Only *three* of the surviving species are still native to the British Isles. This suggests that the clearing of the peat-rich forest beds not only has a disastrous effect upon plants and small animal life, but also upon *larger* animals. All that's left *now* of Norfolk's peaty forests are the *canals*, which have been created through man's pillaging of peat.

The biggest problem of all is that nobody really knows what long-term purpose peat has upon the general welfare of our planet. Nature *never* creates something without *purpose* and we would do well to *remember* that! One thing is *certain* however, it was *not* put there for us to *dig up and destroy!* Peat's natural purpose may be to soak up any excess moisture in times of heavy rainfall, or they may even be there ready for when the polar icecaps melt and raise the levels of the oceans. Maybe they were formed in order to keep the water tables at the right level for the growth of trees and plants. Unfortunately, none of us will be sure of what its original purpose was, until it is *too late!*

OLD KING COAL

Like peat, coal is the ancient remains of plants, trees and animals. Indeed it is even more ancient, since it is formed *from* peat. Hundreds of millions of years ago the earth was a much warmer planet than it is today. The greater part of the land surface was covered with vast forests and jungles. Here, there existed giant ferns and cycads, growing swamps and shallow lagoons. Damp, tropical heat made the surface of the planet like one enormous *hot house*, the *original* 'greenhouse effect'—but this was a part of *nature's plan!* Our present *man-made* 'greenhouse effect' has already caused the deaths of humans and animals, notably during the searing heat wave in Texas in 1998.

As the sun beat relentlessly down upon the Earth's surface, it set up chemical reactions which caused the trees and plants to absorb the carbon, hydrogen and oxygen which caused them to grow to massive heights. When these huge trees and plants died, they fell into swamps and pools, where their remains accumulated into great beds of decaying vegetation. They did not decay *completely* however, due to the acidity of the water. Instead, they became covered in sand and silt until they were completely cut off from the air. They fossilised and nature began laying down the basic safeguards for it's future. Due to the intense heat of the sun, the swamps eventually became bogs, whilst the remains of trees, ferns and mosses became matted together to form the first stage in the process—*peat*. Constant pressure from the materials dying and rotting on top of the more ancient deposits caused these fossils to become compacted so hard that they became *petrified*—rock-like— eventually forming what we know today as *coal*.

The largest deposits of coal are found in Russia, Ireland, Scotland, Canada and the USA. Most of the coal being used with such blind abandon today is thought to have been formed during the *Upper Carboniferous era*, between 200 and 300 million years ago. In those distant times the boundaries between land and sea were not as permanent as they now appear to be. Throughout millions of years new continents and seas were constantly being formed and destroyed. Periodically there were volcanic upheavals and earthquakes frequently shook the Earth. As a result huge areas of forest swamps and peat bogs sank below sea level. They became covered, firstly with water, then with mud, sand and the living shells of sea creatures. Later the seabed would rise again from the force of another earthquake or volcanic eruption. A new island would emerge from the rich deposits of mud, sand and shells and this, in turn, would develop into a new tropical forest. Time and again the sinking and raising of the land would occur, so that alternate layers of vegetation and mud were formed into a 'sandwich'.

At times the peat bogs would become the bottoms of lakes and shallow seas, whilst at *other* times they formed part of an island or a great continent. The shells that had collected on top of the peat would form into rock, hundreds, or even thousands of feet deep. All these successive deposits of peat and rock would exert enormous pressure upon the *lower* deposits of peat. This would slowly become compressed into hard, dry coal. This process, which must have lasted millions of years, forced out of the forming coal deposits the remains of the hydrogen and oxygen that had originally been absorbed by the plants. This left only the carbon. Pressure turned some of this hydrogen and oxygen into highly combustible gases. Large quantities of these gases collected in hollows and pockets in the coal seams. The occasional explosions of these residual gases often cause the disastrous blowouts in the coalmines of today.

Peat, which has not quite turned into coal, is known as *lignite*, from the Latin *lignum*, meaning *wood*. It is like brown coal and consists of some seventy per cent carbon. Lignite is found in large quantities in the USA, Canada, Germany, India, Malaysia, Japan, Australia and New Zealand. In *these* countries it is mined in the same way as coal.

Every year some 1,373,000,000 tons of coal are dig up from coalmines throughout the world, and burned. This is lost to nature forever, due to Mankind's greed and thoughtlessness. Could coal, like peat, have some higher purpose in life? It may act as some sort of insulation, but once again, we won't know until it is too late! Come to that, it is probably too late *already!* In the meantime, coalmining activities have left great holes in The Earth's crust. If all these holes were put together as the *'Holes in Blackburn, Lancashire'* were in the Beatles' classic *A day in the life*, they wouldn't merely fill the *Albert Hall*—they would *create a massive hole the size of the British Isles, at a depth of six feet!* So we have already used 94,272 square miles of coal, at a depth of six feet! It is believed that the Chinese were the first people on Earth to discover the burning capacity of coal some 3,000 years ago. They have a lot to answer for!

Peat and coal when burned emit carbon dioxide into the atmosphere, adding to the 'greenhouse effect'. Normally, plants and trees would absorb much of this carbon dioxide. Unfortunately, we are destroying trees and plants by the hectare and we have been releasing what has been locked away in fossil fuels by carelessly burning coal and peat. We only have ourselves to blame for bringing the *planet itself* to the very edge of extinction! Even so, the damage done by the burning of coal and peat is mild when compared to what *crude oil* and *petroleum products* can do in the hands of Mankind.

Black Gold, Texas Tea

The name *petroleum* comes from the Latin words *petra*, meaning 'rock', and *oleum*, meaning 'oil'. So petroleum literally translates as *'rock oil'*. In it's *natural* form, before being refined and converted into various products, it is known as *crude oil*. 4,000,000,000 years of constant and gradual change in the nature of the Planet Earth has given rise to this natural resource, which Mankind has come to prize so greedily and which now forms the biggest part of the world economy.

It is believed that oil first began forming when vast inland oceans covered much of what is now dry land. These, long since extinct, seas were inhabited by countless millions of tiny sea creatures and underwater plants. As these life forms died, they sank to the bottom of the seas and became buried in the mud of the seabed. More mud, together with sand, which had been carried into the sea by rivers, became deposited on the top of the tombs of these plants and tiny sea creatures. Gradually the weight of the sea itself, together with the weight of the top layers of mud, squeezed the underlying mud into a very hard, coarse stone. This coarse stone is now known as *shale*. Whilst the mud was being transformed into shale, something *else* was happening to the corpses of the sea creatures and plants. They were slowly being transformed into *oil*.

Of course, this took many millions of years, during which time the Earth above was gradually going through changes of it's *own*. Great upheavals were turning rivers on to new courses, drying up inland seas and creating mountains and valleys. All this violent activity on the surface of the planet put tremendous pressure upon the forming oil, which became embedded in its own bed of shale. Eventually this pressure became so great that it squeezed the oil back out of the shale into nearby porous rocks. Once freed from the confinement of the shale, the oil consistently sought its way towards the earth's surface to escape the pressure. On its travels it encountered *other* porous rocks and much of it became absorbed by these. Finally, the remainder of the oil *did* break through the surface, forming what the oil industry now calls 'seepage pools'. More often however, the oil would eventually find its upward journey hindered by a barrier of non-porous rock. At *this* point the oil ceased its travels. In these stone prisons it accumulated. *Not* in vast underground lakes and rivers as some people imagine, but still trapped in the pores of the rock through which it had been travelling.

The small proportion of oil that did reach the surface was soon put to use by early man throughout the world. As the surface of the oil became baked by the sun many prehistoric animals perished in what became known as *tar pits*. The ancient civilisations of Egypt, Persia, India, Mesopotamia and China skimmed oil from these seepage pools to assist in the heating and the lighting of their homes. They also used it for cementing together the stones of their buildings, waterproofing their roofs, caulking the timbers of their ships, surfacing roads and even for waterproofing the wrappings in which they buried their dead! Nobody at *this* time thought of *drilling* for it, or even of *refining* it. They used it exactly as they found it—usually in the form of *bitumen*. The transformation of oil into bitumen is a natural occurrence, caused by the weathering actions of the sun, wind and rain, hence the prehistoric 'tar pits' mentioned earlier.

As time marched ever onwards into the industrial revolution, which began in Britain towards the end of the 18th Century, Mankind developed the power of steam. He now found an increase in the 'need' for oil, for the lubrication of his latest toy—the *steam* engine, *traction* engine and *other* types of machinery. He also needed more of it for the lighting of his factories. In *earlier* times, the *whaling industry* supplied the oil for these needs. As a result, thousands of whales were slaughtered simply for the oil, meat, and most sickening of all, for the bones, which were used in *ladies' corsets!*

In the middle of the 19th Century however, professor *James Young*, a Scots scientist, experimented with ways of refining the crude oil which was seeping into the Derbyshire coal mines. A few years later Young devised a process for extracting oil from shale. Whilst Young was establishing his *shale oil* industry, a small group of American businessmen, upon seeing the commercial potential of oil, engaged a former railway worker called *Edwin Drake* to *drill* for oil in Pennsylvania. Here large oil seepages had been sighted and the businessmen figured that there must be more of it deeper in the ground. After drilling for almost a year they finally struck oil on 27th August 1859, at a depth of about 70 feet. This was the first well to be drilled specifically and successfully for the production of oil as a commercial proposition. The International Oil Industry dates its birth from the date that Drake struck oil on that fateful day. *As you will discover, Edwin Drake and those American businessmen have an awful lot to answer for!*

After drilling *haphazardly* for a while, the new breed of oil men realised that *geologists* might be able to locate the likely positions of underground oil reserves, saving them time and money. Once these sites had been located they figured they could drill for what has become known as 'black gold' or 'Texas tea' with more accuracy. This shows that even from its *earliest* beginnings, the oil industry has relied heavily upon the expertise of scientists. Nowadays bore holes go down as deep as 200,000 feet in the search for oil and it is produced in more than forty different countries. The greatest bulk, however, comes from five main regions: The United States, the Caribbean, the Middle East, the Caspian-Volga-Ural regions of the old USSR, and Indonesia and Borneo in the *Far East*. Now, of course, Mankind even plunders the *seabed* in his insatiable thirst for oil, showing scant concern for the life in the oceans. The oil industry has, in less than 150 years, become the mainstay of world economics—but at *what price?*

CHAPTER NINE:
PAYING THE COST

Like *other* fossil fuels oil burns oxygen and emits carbon dioxide into the atmosphere, depriving ourselves and other creatures of essential oxygen, which we all need merely to *exist*. The carbon dioxide cannot all be absorbed by the Earth's plant life, simply because of the fact that we have destroyed a great percentage of it. This adds to the 'greenhouse effect'. When refined into petrol and used in vehicles it also emits deadly gases such as carbon monoxide, sulphur dioxides and nitrous oxides, all of which are poisonous to plant and animal life alike.

No escape

Oil can also be used for the making of plastics which, when discarded thoughtlessly, adds to the litter which pollutes town, countryside and rivers. There in those places they remain, even if they are buried—for ordinary plastics are not biodegradable—they never rot away. Plastic *containers* and even *sheets* of plastic and plastic *rubbish bags* have *all* caused the deaths of countless numbers of animals and birds, and even our *own children*. They become trapped inside and, as plastic is not porous, they *suffocate*.

Perhaps the *deadliest* threats to the natural environment however, are the *oil spillages* and *oil field fires*. In 1988 the tanker *Exxon Valdez* spilled *eleven million gallons* of oil into the sea off *Alaska*. Twenty-one years earlier in 1967, the *Torry Canyon* spilled *thirty five million gallons* off the coast of *England*. In 1978 the *Amoco Cadiz* spilled *sixty five million gallons* into the sea near *France*. In 1979 the *Atlantic Empress* polluted the coastline of *Trinidad* with *seventy million gallons*. This adds up to *one hundred and eighty one million gallons* of sticky, tar-like, crude oil spilled into the sea within *twenty-one years*. This only accounts for the *larger* spillages from *oil tankers* transporting what the oilmen call 'liquid gold'. Add to this the *eighty million gallons* spilled from the *Norwuz* oil field in the Gulf in 1983, the *eighty million gallons* spilled from the *Ixloc* Oil field in the Gulf of Mexico, and the *three hundred million* from the *Al Ahmed* refinery during the Gulf war of 1991 and you have the makings of a world wide disaster.

All these add up to a staggering total of *six hundred and forty one million gallons* of oil spilled into the sea and consequently washed up onto the shores in just *twenty-four years!* Even so, this figure does *not* take into account the numerous *smaller* spills.

A MATTER OF LIFE OR DEATH

The 1991 oil spill in the Persian Gulf *alone* covered more than *350 square miles* and killed many hundreds of *gulls, cormorants, oystercatchers, curlews, dunlins, redshanks* and *herons*, as well as many rare species of bird such as the *Terek sandpiper* and the *sea plover*.

Death by oil

Legends of *Mermaids* were spawned when ancient mariners, charting the seas in their wooden boats, first discovered these waters and saw, for the first time, the sea cow or *dugong*. To these lonely sailors, who had not *seen*, let alone had *sex* with, a woman for *months* or even *years*, these strange creatures, often hidden behind sea mists, appeared to be half woman and half fish. They even *breast-fed* their young, in a similar manner to human females! Dugongs live inshore around the Gulf and feed upon sea grass. Due to the catastrophic oil spillages during the Gulf war the dugong may well become totally extinct in this region. Oddly enough, scientists now track these creatures by way of satellite, attaching radio transmitters to their heads, but I do wonder whether this practice does more harm than good—alienating them from their fellow creatures or making them prime targets for predators! *Maybe we are interfering too much in trying to put right the balance!*

The slick caught fire causing an even *greater* environmental hazard. Then *Saddam Hussein*, as part of his 'scorched earth' policy, deliberately set fire to at least *two hundred Kuwaiti oilfields*. Ships more than fifty miles offshore became enveloped in thick black smog. The sun was blotted out from sight and the smell of sulphur filled the air. The cloud brought with it *acid rain*, which poisoned the water supplies for thousands of miles around the Gulf. Acid rain is not only lethal to *plant and animal life*, it caused *soot* to fall over the mountains of Iran causing the snows to melt early. We did not fully appreciate the full extent of the damage to the environment until years later, but it has almost certainly added to the *El Nino* phenomenon and the current problems with the Earth's climate.

This area used to *teem* with wildlife, supporting many species of marine animals, fish and plants, many of which were quite common though others were quite rare. Whatever the loss, much of it can *never* be replaced. All the flora and fauna of the sea were suffocating and every single organism was under threat. As the oil spilled into the sea, as one reporter put it, 'it did not even sound like the waves of the *ocean* any more. The oil was so thick that the water could hardly build up into waves *at all*. It sounded more like *gurgling mud* than the roar of waves crashing against the shore.' No longer did the sea *wash* the beaches as nature *intended*, instead it *defiled* them with *black tar* and *sticky oil*.

Apart from the *birds* and the *dugongs*, many *dolphins* and *turtles* perished, along with countless small crustaceans such as *shrimps*. Some of the birds, which escaped suffocation, died *anyway* because their basic *foods*, fish and crustaceans, had been *poisoned*. Up to *two million* migrating birds suffered a slow and painful death in the world's worst-ever single environmental disaster. It had been unleashed by just *one* country—*Iraq*—for purely selfish reasons, in the name of war.

Closer to home, the oil tanker *Braer* spilled *85,000 tons* of oil into the sea around the Shetland coastline in 1993. This spillage spelt disaster for the grey and common seals and their six-week old pups, as well as sea otters, shags, long-tailed ducks, black guillemots, eider ducks, red-breasted mergansers, scaups, great northern divers, salmon, crabs, mussels and other shellfish. An even *bigger* ecological disaster was avoided by the onset of huge sea storms, which evaporated much of the oil.

In February 1996 the oil tanker *Sea Empress* spilled more than *one million gallons* of crude oil when it hit rocks at St Annes Head, near Milford Haven in West Wales. This happened at a time when almost 3,000 birds were coming ashore to breed on the cliffs around the coast. The spill affected 20,000 guillemots, razorbills and puffins, 100,000 pairs of shearwaters, 28,000 pairs of gannets and 20,000 pairs of seagulls. 5,000 grey seals and hundreds of porpoises were also hit by the oil slick.

The sad fact is that it has continued into this century. In November 2002 the oil tanker *Prestige* sank off the coast of Spain taking with it *77,000 tonnes* of heavy fuel oil, much of which has been leaking into the sea ever since. The fishing port of Caion in Galicia, once rich in shellfish and octopus, has been turned into what the locals call the *Coast of Death*. Within a week *9,000 tonnes* of this oil had spread to the Cornish coast of Cawsand Bay, where rescue workers worked around the clock to clean the oil off the feathers of marine creatures such as seals, and sea birds such as guillemots and puffins. *This, and all the other oil spillages that I have catalogued here could continue seeping into the oceans of the world for many centuries to come.*

More recently, at just after 6am on Sunday 11th December 2005, a number of explosions took place at the Buncefield Oil Depot at Leverstock Green, near Hemel Hempstead, where they supply the aviation fuel to nearby Luton and Heathrow airports, as well as to petrol pumps across the region. At our house in Stevenage, approximately 20 miles away, we heard the explosions, which woke my family and myself up.

Buncefield

It transpired that *sixty million gallons* of oil were ignited, spewing toxic clouds across 1,500 square miles, stretching to a length of 200 miles of the British countryside, putting at risk milk and water supplies due to 'black rain' contaminating grass, rivers and reservoirs, as well as the health of millions of animals and people across Britain. It took the fire brigade more than three days to bring the fire under control. All this makes you wonder doesn't it, if the oil would have been better left where nature had intended—*locked up safely beneath the earth in porous rocks.*

Why then, we may ask ourselves, if oil is such an obvious hazard to the planet is it so prized by Mankind and allowed to become the basis of world economy? In 1965 the British Government, under the premiership of Edward Heath, banned *cigarette* commercials from television on the grounds that smoking was found to be injurious to health. It is beyond comprehension then, that the advertising of *cars and petrol products,* which have been proved to be disastrous for the *whole planet,* is not only *allowed* but also actually *encouraged!* I have written to successive governments about this anomaly and also to the various watchdogs on television standards. I have been totally ignored, or treated as a crank.

A certain TV commercial, which told us that a certain make of car 'takes your breath away', was chillingly accurate. The one that told us 'it needn't cost the Earth' was *way* off the mark! Yet the motor trade and petrochemical industries remain the richest and most profitable in the world! I have tried to get published several articles on this subject, one of which was titled, quite appropriately, 'The Great Oil Conspiracy'. Several newspapers and magazines, many of which had happily taken less controversial articles over a period of years, have turned it down. It was also turned down as a subject for a *television programme.* Very often, when writing letters to the local newspapers, they have seen fit to 'edit out the controversial bits'.

For instance, when the Hemel Hempstead oil disaster occurred, I wrote to the British newspaper *The Daily Mirror* expressing my concerns that oil had been taken from the Earth in the *first* place. 'As an environmentalist I believe that we should never have taken oil out of the ground in the first place: it took nature billions of years to lay down and just over 100 years for humans to practically deplete it. *What if nature had a REASON for putting oil there, such as to guard the Earth from Global Warming, or to oil the tectonic plates? What fools humans are!'* They printed it in full, except for the last two sentences (in italics)—well, what a surprise! The reasons were obvious to *me*— it would upset the *advertisers and sponsors* who help *pay* for those publications and programmes!

One particular well-known gardening magazine published my articles for *years* whilst they were championing *organic* gardening. With a new editor came a new policy. They started taking advertisements from the big *chemical companies* and my articles were dropped like hot potatoes!

Huge profits are made by the advertising industry through newspapers, magazines and commercial television. In fact, there are more advertising campaigns for motor vehicles and petrochemical products than for any other single commercial enterprise. Huge amounts of money are spent on these. Newspapers, magazines, commercial radio and television, and the advertising industry *itself* would soon go *bankrupt* if it were not for the revenue coming in from the motor and petrochemical industries.

You will notice too, that, more often than not, the 'star prize' on any TV game show or newspaper competition is a 'brand new car'. It is little wonder that my more 'controversial' articles get rejected! Never mind about the future of the *planet,* who is going to bite the hands that *feed* them?

Another reason why it is dangerous to knock the oil industry is that the 'developed' countries have become so dependent upon the motor and petrochemical industries that their whole economy is *based* upon it. Forget *bullion* and *sterling,* the *real* world currency on the stock market today is *oil!*

So why, you may ask, don't the scientists, who have previously been relied upon to warn us of impending peril and global catastrophe, speak out honestly and openly about the disastrous effects of oil and petrol products upon our one and only home in the universe? As I have already explained, many of these scientists are actually *employed* by the motor and petrochemical industries! Scientists are only human and, as this book hammers home in no uncertain terms, human beings are notoriously greedy and self-centred!

The late *Paul Foot*, the investigative journalist who was sacked from the British newspaper *The Daily Mirror* for telling the truth, uncovered a plot by the oil companies at the very heart of British

Government. According to *Mr Foot*, in March 1979, during the last days of the then Labour Government in Britain, *Robert Adley*, MP for Lymington, moved an amendment to the Merchant Shipping Bill in the House of Commons. His new clause would have made oil companies responsible for oil spillages at sea. In his speech he quoted the massive oil pollution that had occurred that month from the wrecked tanker *Braer* in the Shetland Islands. He was well supported. Everybody on the Standing Committee on the bill voted for his clause except the Minister, *Stanley Clinton-Davis*, and the Government Whip, *John Evans*. The amendment was carried, 10 votes to 2.

Prime Minister *Jim Callaghan* and Leader of the Opposition, *Margaret Thatcher*, were both under intense pressure from the oil companies to remove the clause. A few days later the Labour Government fell and all non-controversial Bills in Committee were stampeded through the Commons. *Mr. Adley* was summoned to 10 Downing Street to see *Jim Callaghan*. *Mr Callaghan* told *Adley*, 'the only way that bill can get onto the Statute Book is if you will agree to have that clause removed without any further discussion. Otherwise, the Bill will fail.' *Robert Adley* had no alternative but to agree to this pressure and the clause was removed. As a result the oil companies are *still* not held legally responsible for oil spillages at sea! *Mr. Adley* told *Paul Foot* in 1993 when the story came out, 'if the oil companies were made responsible for the pollution which is caused by their oil, they would be very much more careful about chartering leaky old tubs to put it in.' *Paul Foot* asked *Mr Adley* why it was that both major party leaders had opposed his clause in 1979. 'I'll tell you who runs this country,' *Mr Adley* was reported as saying, 'it's the *oil companies!*' Who can disagree with *that?* Unfortunately, it's the same the world over.

In Britain in 2005 a new wave of hooliganism took over the streets, with 'happy slapping' becoming popular with young hooligans. This actually meant beating up people purely for the 'fun' of it, so it was hardly *'happy'* for the victim! It was blamed upon 'hoodies' — youngsters who wore hooded coats, which just happened to be the fashion at the time, made popular by British footballers like David

Beckham. Many authorities began to 'ban' the hooded coats from shopping malls!

Well, personally, I have no doubt that the reason why people are becoming more aggressive and anti-social is because they are breathing in more and more carbon monoxide (which causes brain damage) from traffic fumes, and a diet of junk food and additives, which ALSO mess with the brain! Over the past forty years I have witnessed generations of latchkey kids, who sit on the kerb awaiting the return of their parents, rather than going in to an empty house. They often play 'kerbsy', which means that, sitting on the kerb, they are in exactly the right position for maximum inhalation of the brain-damaging carbon monoxide from motor vehicles. Witness too, young mothers crossing the road with their children in buggies: They push them out into the road behind passing vehicles and again the child is at exactly the right level to breathe in the maximum of motor fumes!

Since the fifties not only has there been an increase in traffic and pollution, but there has also been an increase in food additives, some of which, like *aspartame* (found in diet drinks and artificial sweeteners), can actually cause brain damage! Junk food too causes disruptive behaviour. So, by expanding our towns, we will be causing more pollution and at the same time, in destroying trees, cutting off our natural oxygen supply from the green plants and trees that will be destroyed. *We are actually suffocating ourselves!*

All is not lost however, for there *are* alternatives to all the products that cause us so many problems. There *are* ways of turning the *Vandals in the Garden* into loving, caring, responsible inhabitants of *This Garden Earth*. Unfortunately, the odds against this happening causes me and my fellow environmentalists to sit down, head in hand, *CRYING FOR THE EARTH...*

CHAPTER TEN:
CRYING FOR THE EARTH...

If a superior, intelligent life form from some far-off galaxy should visit the planet Earth after studying our previous history, they would regard Mankind as being in his 'early teenage years' as far as intellect was concerned. I must say—*I would agree!*

Our imaginary aliens would observe World Statesmen trying to appear 'adult' with all the pomp and gobbledegook that goes with the political profession of any persuasion and of any nationality. *Children playing at being adults!* They talk about the problems of world poverty and pollution, whilst at the same time, gorging themselves on state banquets, drilling for oil and mining for coal and minerals. They tell us we should all travel by public transport, cycle or walk, whilst going everywhere *themselves* by 'gas-guzzling' cars. At the same time, they whoop with glee as our car exports reach new heights. They tell us that we must look after the environment, whilst planning the destruction of huge areas of countryside in order to build housing estates and motorways. They order the 'beautification' of old mining sites (as in Britain's *National Forest* project), whilst at the same time ordering the rape of the Earth for coal, peat and precious and non-precious metals.

They continue to allow the land, sea and air to become polluted with oil and chemicals, whilst apparently showing concern over the latest Man-made environmental disaster. They show concern over violence amongst young people and society in general, whilst waging war upon their fellow human beings. They continue to lay claim to a piece of land that was never theirs, but belonged to *nature* in the *first* place! They quote peace and harmony from their own religious 'bible', whilst allowing people to be killed, in the *name* of that religion!

Our visitors would *know* that living on a planet as beautiful as Earth is a privilege that could be taken away at any time. They would see that the economies of all the 'powerful' countries of this planet are based upon the single biggest pollutant of all—*oil*, and that the leaders of those countries have no intention of giving it up, whatever they might say in public. Indeed, they would wonder *why* we have to split the world up into countries and nationalities, rather than *all* being inhabitants of *one world*.

They would see a planet governed by small-minded patriots, hypocrites, egotists, religious fanatics and despots, people who are more interested in their own personal power than in the welfare of their planet and all the life that lives upon it. They would see leaders of confusion. Children playing with toys that they barely understand. Mankind using nuclear power, for example, is like a baby finding a box of matches and trying to find out what it can do. *A recipe for disaster!*

Looking back at the recent history of Mankind, they would discover that a specially designed aircraft was sent to fly across the North Pole equipped with all the latest 'high-tech' equipment. Its mission was to test the diminishing ozone layer, to find out how much damage had been done by our use of CFCs and *other* pollutants. It really wouldn't take our imaginary 'super intelligence' to figure out that, by using a jet aircraft to study the ozone layer, the very craft they were using was actually causing *more damage!*

Every year the polar bears of the Arctic, after starving for months whilst giving birth to cubs, make their way on to the ice shelf for their staple diet of seal meat. They pound at the ice, where the seals hide, until it breaks and they drag the seal out for food ... until *2005* that is! In that year, because of global warming, the sea was not freezing over, which meant there was no ice for the bears to walk on in search of their prey. This means many Polar Bears, and their cubs, are dying of starvation—so what did the 'conservationists' do about it? Well, believe it or not, they travelled out there *IN GIANT-WHEELED PETROL-DRIVEN VEHICLES* to investigate the problem! Didn't they realise that petrol fumes are only *ADDING TO THE PROBLEM? I DESPAIR!!!*

In order to 'help' wildlife, scientists and conservationists use 'modern technology' to track these animals and birds. They tie transmitters to them, which sends a signal to a satellite way out in space and beams it back to earth, so that the scientists can keep a track on what is happening to the wildlife. The problem here is that these transmitters, however small, are cumbersome for the creature and can affect its movements (particularly in the case of birds and sea creatures). It can mean these creatures are easily spotted by any animals that prey on them (including humans!). Also, they may well affect the delicate navigational signals that wild creatures use and of which we know very little about!

Professing to 'protect our wildlife' these conservationists, prior to fitting them with these abominable devices, trap them in what they call 'humane traps', which are humane only in *our* eyes! Just imagine our alien visitors trapping *us* in 'Humane Traps'—don't you think that we would get panicky and distressed? Well, so do the animals, birds, fish and even insects. The fact that they (as far as we know) cannot reason in the same way that we do, makes it even *worse*, for they act upon instinct and naturally believe that they are being trapped in order to be eaten. It is even possible that they may be targeted by their own species due to the human scent upon them!

For the same dubious purposes, these scientists shoot drug-filled darts into larger, or more 'dangerous' animals such as lions and tigers, which paralyze them in order for the scientists to examine them, or fit them with remote devices. How would *we* like to be paralyzed and be at the mercy of our hypothetical aliens? So are these scientists *really* doing it to help wildlife, or are they doing it for *themselves?*

It seems that whatever modern Man does, it affects, in some way, the planet and the creatures that live upon it.

* * * * * *

What kind of intelligent life form would deliberately put their own planet in peril and slaughter countless numbers of their fellow creatures as they engage in primitive 'tribal warfare'?

WHEN TWO TRIBES GO TO WAR...

The *first* World War lasted for a period of four years from 1914 AD to 1918 AD. In that short time we managed to kill and maim *thirty million people!*

During the *second* World War, between 1939 AD and 1945 AD, 307,210 soldiers were killed in the British armed services alone, whilst 60,585 *civilians* were killed during the 'blitz' on London. About 50,000 civilians were killed during the allied invasion upon Berlin and several million German and Russian soldiers were killed on the Eastern Front. Possibly the most appalling figure of all was the 70,000 Japanese civilians who were killed by the atomic bomb that was dropped by the Americans on 6th August 1945. In 1998, when the emperor of Japan visited Britain, First World War veterans had the cheek to turn their backs on him, because *they* didn't apologise to *us* for *their* atrocities! It just goes to show how dangerous patriotism is—and it is peculiar to Mankind!

It has been estimated that *one hundred million people* have been killed in wars during the twentieth century alone. *That is exactly a third of the world's population as it was, during the great Egyptian civilization four thousand years ago.*

How many *animals, birds, fish and insects* have been killed, maimed or sent mad during wartime is *anyone's* guess, as Mankind is far too *selfish* to bother with *these* estimates. It is likely to number in *billions* however, judging by the number of casualties during the strange barbaric British Festival known as *bonfire night!* Many of my friends from other countries are somewhat bemused by the fact that we British celebrate a *failed* attempt to blow up Parliament! In my opinion *success* would have been a better cause for celebration!

Cats, dogs and hedgehogs in particular have been known to die, or suffer serious injuries during this barbaric festival and many household pets have to be given sedatives to keep them calm. My own dog, Majick, had to be sedated almost constantly for about a month before and after bonfire night, because of the non-stop explosions. This, together with other factors, leads me to the known conclusion that we don't keep pets for the love of the *animal* but for our *own* satisfaction. Difficult as it may be for us to accept, we don't really *love* our pets, we love the idea of *owning* them—but more about this later.

Imagine the effect loud noises like fireworks, let alone *bombs*, must have upon *wild* animals and birds, that do not have anyone to sedate them!

It amazes me too, especially during the constant terror alert following the ill-fated Gulf War of the mid 2000s, that every year shops are allowed to supply explosives to the general public on the open market in the form of fireworks! *I wonder what our alien friends would make of that?*

The Gulf War of 1991 lasted for only 43 days, commencing on 16th January 1991, yet 100,000 Iraqis alone were killed, including 500 women and children who died when the allied forces bombed a Baghdad shelter. The allied forces themselves got away very lightly, though the *Americans* managed to kill nine young soldiers when they mistakenly attacked the *British armoured carriers!* This is not the first time the Americans have killed their own or allied forces. They did it during the Second World War and also in Vietnam. They've even done it during *training exercises!* Considering the fact that the Americans were accused of only going into the Gulf War because of their interests in *Kuwaiti oil,* this didn't do anything to *improve* their image! Add to this the fact that, after inciting the Kurds to rise up against Saddam Hussein, the Americans, under the leadership of *George Bush*, didn't lift a finger when the Iraqi 'Elite Guard' retaliated and began slaughtering the Kurdish people! Could this be because there was no *profit* involved? Only after great international public outcry did the USA and Great Britain send aid to the refugees. Since then of course, Tony Blair and George W Bush have taken us into another war in Iraq, mentioned earlier—one which wasn't even recognized by the United Nations and which, still to this day, is regarded by many (including myself) as illegal under International law. Yet *still* they get away with it!

IF WE COULD TALK TO THE ANIMALS...

If, like Dr. Doolittle, we could talk to the animals, what do you think they would tell us? We regard them as 'dumb creatures'—but *are* they? They may well be smarter than *us!*

For a start the wild animals, birds, fish and insects would obviously object to us robbing them of their homes so that we can build homes for *ourselves*. Foxes, deer, hares and many *other* creatures wouldn't think much of us pursuing them on horseback, with a pack of baying hounds and tearing them to pieces in the name of sport. Neither would fish agree to being caught on a hook and thrown back into the rivers and seas to suffer for our 'pleasure'.

Unfortunately, the bloodlust is so deeply rooted in us, especially the 'gentry' as we call it in this country, that even when the law is changed (as it was in September 2005 to prevent foxes, deer, hares, etc, being torn about by hounds and followed by bloodthirsty hunters on horseback) the gentry feel they are far above the law and so continually break it. On Boxing Day 2005 huntsmen openly flouted the law and went ahead with their bloodthirsty 'sport' as though nothing had changed.

I am sure animals would object to traps, snares, insecticides and *other* chemicals, which either kill them *directly* or *indirectly*. I am absolutely sure that wild animals would be happier living a natural life in the wild than being ogled by people in zoos and circuses, but what of our *pets* and *domesticated* animals? I doubt that horses would willingly give up their freedom for being ridden by humans, or being made to pull heavy carts and farm equipment. Neither would llamas, mules, camels and reindeer wish to carry heavy loads for the benefit of Mankind. Racehorses are so brainwashed by their human 'masters' that they will run a race in any circumstances. It is quite common, in fact, for racehorses to run at the bidding of their trainers, owners and jockeys, even when they are very ill. Some have actually died of a heart attack on the racecourse. Indeed, in October 2005, Triple Cheltenham Gold Cup winner *Best Mate* died on the racetrack after he collapsed while running in The William Hill Haldon Gold Cup at

Caged eagle

Exeter. The horse, trained by Henrietta Knight, seemed to be in some distress after being pulled up by jockey Paul Carberry. But as he was being brought back to the course stables he collapsed with a suspected heart attack and died. "I think he died doing what he enjoyed doing," said trainer Knight. Well, I beg to differ, he actually died doing what *they* loved him to do—*making money for them!*

Huskies too, those sturdy dogs that have been specially bred by Mankind to pull sledges, will run and run until they drop dead—such is the unnatural instincts we have bred into them. They only do it because we force our will upon them, just as we have done with *human* slaves over the centuries. For make no mistake about this, these animals are our slaves to do our bidding and have to be trained or broken in by us humans from an early age in order to break them of their natural, wild spirits.

Let's face it, we even talk of 'owning' pets, as did rich folk talk in days gone by of 'owning' slaves! They are NOT pets, they are possessions, because people love to own and possess things! Dogs, cats, fish and birds have been especially bred by Mankind to satisfy a whim—to make them different from their wild ancestors, to show everyone else how clever we are, or how rich we are, by owning something that is different! As a result many breeds have developed abnormal characteristics such as pug noses (as in bulldogs and suchlike), which cause breathing difficulties, and unnatural growths and eye positioning, as in lionhead and celestial goldfishes. The sickest part of it is that the owners proudly display these monstrosities in shows, where they hope to win a certificate for these unnatural abominations!

Cows, sheep, pigs and *other* farm animals wouldn't choose to live on a farm awaiting the slaughterhouse if they were given the option and neither would chickens choose to live in battery farms and being turned into egg-producing factories! Ah! I hear you cry, but these are *farm* animals, we all love our *pets*, don't we? *Do we?*

Probably the only 'pets' that are quite *happy* with their lot are *cats*—providing they are not ill-treated. We feed them and they can keep warm in front of the fire when they choose to do so, otherwise a cat will come and go as it pleases and lead the life that suits it best. Even so, there is *one* practice that humans impose upon them, which breaches the rights of all living things—they get '*spayed*' or '*doctored*'! Neutering, in one form or the other, is practised on *dogs* and *other* pets and farm animals too, not only to prevent them from following their natural instincts in breeding, but also in order to curb their natural tendencies for aggression and body odour. How selfish is *that?* I wonder how *humans* would feel if our 'super intelligence' decided they would neuter *us* because there were *too many humans* on the Earth (which there undoubtedly *is*)? Even the *thought* of owning other life forms should be *abhorrent* to any *really* intelligent life form. Which just goes to show you how far we still have to travel along the evolutionary path. Even dogs and farm animals that are *not* 'doctored' seldom get the chance to follow their natural instincts with the opposite sex, because we keep them in our houses or in fenced-off fields and only take them or allow them out under *our* supervision and *our* rules. Would cats, dogs and farm animals agree to *this*, given the chance? I *doubt* it!

When it comes down to it, whether or not we say we love our pets, the truth is that we love to *own* our pets. Whichever way you look at it, *it is slavery*. We *own* our pets in the same way that we own our house, car, stereo—whatever—and we really have no right at all to *own any living creature!*

Police dogs are expected to lay their lives on the line for us when they chase criminals or sniff for drugs or bombs, but nobody ever *asked* them if they wanted to serve Mankind in this way!

The slavery of fellow humans was abolished, quite rightly, many years ago—so why is it still legal to own animals?

Would a *goldfish* or *tropical fish* choose to swim around in constant circles in the confines of an aquarium if it were given the chance to escape to a nice fresh *river?* Would a bird willingly give up a life in the wild for the confines of a cage or aviary? Some birds, such as hawks and falcons, are allowed a certain amount of freedom to scare off or destroy birds that humans don't want in their 'private' domain. These unfortunate creatures are tethered with leather straps and released only in order to do their 'master's' bidding. The straps are left dangling from the leg of the bird when they are released, creating a hazard which could easily become entangled on a tree branch or fence and causing the bird great suffering. Many are even fitted with radio transmitters so that the 'master' can keep track of them! Unfortunately, these birds have been 'trained' (or more to the point, 'brainwashed') into doing the bidding of their masters—and we dare to call ourselves civilized!

The same can be said of any *number* of pets from rabbits and hamsters to snakes and terrapins—so don't tell me that we keep pets because we *love* them! What we *really* love, if we were totally *honest*, is keeping them in our own private little zoos as our own personal *possessions!*

Finally, would any intelligent human being think for one minute that animals raised in laboratories actually *like* the idea of being used to test *drugs, cosmetics* and the effects of *smoking?* Do they like the idea of being given *cancer* and *other* diseases? Would they actually opt for having *human parts* grafted onto their skin; or being exposed to *radiation*; have their *genes tampered with*; or have *clones* of themselves made? Hardly! I suspect that, maybe in a few hundred years from now (assuming that humans or the planet *survive* that long), our future generations will look back on our history and will be appalled at the fact that we owned and used animals the way we do today. I certainly hope so, for it will at last be a sign that Mankind is eventually growing up and regarding our co-inhabitants of this planet with the respect they deserve.

WHEN THE PLANET FIGHTS BACK...

When disease-causing viruses and bacteria attack your body, your body's defences are put upon alert. There are *white blood cells* and *antibodies*, which actually attack any foreign body that may enter the body. If your body is in danger of *overheating* the *sweat glands* work overtime in an effort to keep you *cool* and if you are *cold* the body causes you to *shiver* in an effort to produce *energy and heat*. If your *skin* is cut *platelets* in the blood rush to the spot in an effort to seal up the wound. In fact, *every* living organism has a *defence mechanism* to protect it from harm and the planet Earth is no different.

Mankind has been abusing their home planet for so long it's inevitable that it would fight back. It is an automatic mechanism, designed to preserve the planet itself and all the other life upon it. This may be seen clearly in the results of our constant pollution of the air, land and waters. Not only is the air becoming *unbreathable,* the waters *undrinkable* and the land *poisoned,* but the whole weather patterns across the globe are becoming unstable. This has led to the depletion of the *ozone layer,* which protects us from the harmful rays of the sun. No longer is it safe to 'sunbathe' for fear of developing *skin cancer,* which is on the increase throughout the world. Our actions have also caused what scientists call the *greenhouse effect,* which will eventually raise the mean temperatures of the Earth to dangerous levels.

In the *meantime* however, our weather systems are becoming notoriously *unstable*. The phenomenon, which scientists have named *El Nino,* has been brought into play by the planet itself as a warning to the perpetrators—*us! El Nino* is the name given to a southward-flowing ocean current off the coasts of Peru and Ecuador. Cyclical changes in the pattern of its flow are the cause of environmental and climatic disturbances that cause widespread damage every few years. It was given the name *El Nino*, which means *'The Child'*, as a reference to Jesus Christ by the Spanish, as the current usually appears around Christmastime.

The *El Nino* current normally flows south from the Eastern Equatorial Countercurrent and then converges with the Northward Peru Current a few degrees south of the Equator. Atmospheric disturbances, such as those triggered off by the 1982 eruption of Mexico's *El Chichon* volcano, cause it to occasionally extend further along the Peruvian coast. *El Nino's* warm and nutrient-poor waters can cause great damage to the environment. The climatic effects of large scale *El Nino* disturbances can cause flooding and drought conditions over a wide area, sometimes extending as far as the southern Pacific Ocean, Europe, Africa and Asia.

There is now evidence that Man's interference with the atmosphere, through nuclear explosions, aircraft and rocket disturbances and atmospheric pollution in general, is causing more and more *El Nino* disturbances and they have become more active since atomic testing became commonplace during the 'cold war' in the nineteen-fifties. Such disturbances have taken place in 1953, 1957/58, 1972/73, 1976, 1982/83, 1992 and then almost continuously from 1996 to 1999, and then into the Twenty-first Century. Indeed, Global Warming seems to be causing this phenomenon to become a permanent feature. In the latter part of the nineteen-nineties alone, *El Nino* wreaked havoc right across the globe.

To make matters worse, *El Nino* spawned a little sister *La Nina* (*Little girl*), the name given to a huge belt of cold water on the Pacific Equator. Warmer water occurs north and south of the cold water, which snuffles out rain clouds above it but drags rain clouds in its wake. Together, *El Nino* and *La Nina* have caused unprecedented flooding in New Zealand, torrential rain in Australia and freezing conditions in Chile and further up the coast of South America. In October/November 1998, *Hurricane Mitch* caused the deaths of 20,000 people in Central America. Floods killed 5,000 in Honduras and 1,500 died in Nicaragua when part of a volcano collapsed, causing a massive landslide. All in all, over one million people were made homeless.

In Britain, April 1998 was the wettest in 180 years and *one month's* average rain fell in *twenty-four hours* in the south midlands just before the Easter weekend. In January of the same year winds reached *one hundred miles per hour* in Cornwall and in the same month a *tornado* hit Selsey, West Sussex, causing damage to 1,000 properties. Other, lesser, tornadoes hit various parts of Britain in the same year. Wales and the Midlands suffered their worst floods in living memory in October 1998.

Belgium suffered its worst floods for almost a century in September 1998. More than *one hundred and fifty people* died in *Texas, USA*, due to a *two-month heat wave* during June/July 1998 where the temperatures reached 120F. The heat wave also affected Washington and Philadelphia where temperatures remained above 100F for over a month. Whilst *Papua, New Guinea* was hit by a *giant tidal wave*, caused by an *undersea earthquake* eighteen miles off the coast. There were waves measuring up to *thirty feet*, which crashed across *28 miles of land*, killing *1600 people directly* and over *6,000* in all, due to the resulting diseases which followed.

In July 1998 the *Yangtze River* in *China* burst it's banks and flooded the Sichuan Province, killing almost three thousand people. More than 1,000 people died in *Bangladesh* when that country experienced the worst flooding in recorded history and 70% of the land was under water by September 1998. *Also* in September 1998 *Hurricane Georges* ripped through *Antigua, The Caribbean, Florida, The Gulf of Mexico* and *New Orleans*. By the end of September it had killed more than *300 people*.

All these disasters happened in *one year*—1998—the year, according to meteorologists, in which the Earth's mean temperature was the highest for over *one thousand years*.

As we entered the new Millennium another spate of unprecedented 'natural' disasters began. On Boxing Day, 16th December 2004 a tsunami (giant wave caused by a submarinal earthquake) hit several communities on the coast of the Indian Ocean, killing a total of *188,000 – 80,000* in Indonesia alone. *Hurricane Katrina*, the first of a record number of hurricanes in the Gulf Coast, hit Miami, Florida on 25th August 2005 and then went on to cause even greater damage to New Orleans on 29th August. It caused the levees to breach, creating apocalyptic flooding and killing *1,342 people*. It was said to be the most destructive hurricane in the history of the USA. On 8th October 2005 a huge earthquake hit Southern Asia killing *about 73,000 people* in Pakistan *and 1,300* in India. Then three days later, on 11th October, *Hurricane Stan* killed *800 people* in Guatemala.

On Thursday October 1st 1998 *The World Wide Fund for Nature* published *The Living Planet*, a report which warned that Earth's natural resources had been reduced by *one third over the past 25 years* and we have destroyed, during that same period, *10 percent of the world's forests*. I could have *told* them this from my *own* findings over the past *40 years!*

Global warming may seem attractive to many as temperatures in the UK rise to sub-tropical levels, for example. This also means, however, that many creatures not previously *existing* in Britain are now *thriving*. The malaria-carrying mosquito, *Anopheles algeriensis*, has been sighted in *Anglesey*. *Banana spiders*, which can bite, have been imported into Britain with crates of bananas from Brazil and are thriving here. *Bee-wolf wasps*, which attack and paralyse our native honeybee, have been sighted in *Essex* and the *Isle of Wight*. *Scorpions* are becoming well established in *Harwich*, *Colchester*, and *Sheerness* on the Isle of Sheppey. *Other* alien insects making a home in Britain include the *American cockroach*, the *Colorado beetle*, *Eurowasps*, which carry potentially lethal stings, *Greenhouse spiders*, which look like a black widow and can bite, and the *Parasitic wasp*, which can infect 200 ladybirds during it's three-week lifespan.

On our *seashores* there are more dangers, as those taking up residence include the *compass jellyfish* whose sting can cause severe illness for up to 48 hours and sharks, such as the great white, which can cause potential danger to swimmers.

Our actions are causing the *ice caps* at the Earth's poles to melt and this in turn will cause the *sea levels* to rise across the globe, reducing the *earth's landmasses* dramatically. *polar bears* are in real danger of becoming *totally extinct*, not only because of the rising temperatures as mentioned earlier, but also because they eat *seals,* which eat *fish* that have been contaminated with *industrial pollutants*. Native Inuit (once known as Eskimos) are finding it more and more difficult to go about their normal traditional hunting methods because the ice in some places can no longer support the weight of their sleds.

In December 2005 an Anglo-American team, studying the effects of global warming in the Antarctic, published a map showing exactly how much damage has been done to The West Antarctic Ice Sheet. This is a critical piece of the jigsaw that makes up the whole picture of the effects of Global Warming, where many scientists warn of the rapid collapse of the shelf, which, in turn, could submerge the World's coastal cities and wipe out *ten percent of the population!* Amazingly, in order to gather this information, the team of scientists who carried out the *research SPENT TWO MONTHS FLYING BACKWARDS AND FORWARDS OVER THE AREA!* ONCE AGAIN, DIDN'T IT OCCUR TO THEM THAT BY DOING THIS THEY WERE ACTUALLY *ADDING* TO THE PROBLEM? *This just goes to prove how ignorant Mankind really is of the actual effects his activities are having upon this planet!*

It has also been noted that the hole in the ozone layer over the Antarctic is closing much slower than scientists had predicted since the ban on the use of Chlorofluorocarbons (CFCs) in refrigerators in 1987. The delay is now being blamed on old fridges and air conditioning systems, which should have been banned, still in use.

Depletion of the ozone layer is blamed for exposure to harmful ultraviolet radiation, which is known to cause skin cancer and cataracts.

Many polar bears are becoming *sterile* and the *sperm count* amongst *human* males is now half what it was in the nineteen-fifties. It could be that Mankind will no longer be capable of *reproducing* by the middle of the twenty-first century, causing *our* extinction too!

The way forward

What with all of Mankind's selfishness, war, the pollution of land, sea and air, the decimation of our forests, countryside and wildlife, the wholesale theft of the Earths resources and the 'ownership' of animals, could our hypothetical space travellers consider anything less than exterminating the entire Human Race in order to save the planet as a whole? *Only* if we change our ways *dramatically!*

We could begin by allowing cultures, which are different to our own (North American Natives, forest people of the rainforests, The Inuit, the nomadic tribes of Arabia and Lapland, the Aborigines, for example), to live their lives without our interference either culturally or religiously. We could produce electricity by means of wind power, wave power or solar energy, allowing us to cut down and eventually stop using fossil fuels completely. We could develop a means of transport that uses electricity, solar energy, or even water!

Transport

The Russians actually developed an *aircraft* in 1990 that uses *water* as a *power source.* In 1991 the British newspaper, *The Daily Mirror* predicted that the water-powered *car* would be available by 1993 after an American computer and hydrogen expert, *Dr Roger Billings*, invented a revolutionary fuel cell, the *Laser Cell-TM*, especially for the purpose of extracting hydrogen from water. As we all know, the chemical make-up of water is H_2O—hydrogen and oxygen. At the heart of the hydro car is *Dr. Billings'* fuel cell, which takes the hydrogen out of the water and converts it into electricity. The power produced propels an electric engine. *Simple* really! In *this* form of

Hydroelectric power

transport, *two gallons of water* would provide enough hydrogen for a *300-mile journey* and the car could travel in excess of 80 miles per hour. The engine is only a third the size of a conventional petrol engine and, as it has no moving parts, it would last for more than 250,000 miles needing virtually no servicing! Whatever *happened* to that? Well, at the time, a New York analyst summed it up *this* way, "Billings' breakthrough is of tremendous interest, but that doesn't mean that motor manufacturers will all be rushing to convert to hydrogen. I'm afraid that vested interests will make the path to hydrogen cars a very difficult one." It looks as though that analyst was right. Never mind about saving the *planet*—let's all keep on *lining our pockets!*

For many years a device similar to Billings' *fuel cell* has been *another* real option to the internal combustion engine, but consecutive governments have been bypassing it for generations, probably, once again, through 'vested interests'. The fuel cell is a kind of battery that instead of recharging with *electricity* you recharge its *chemicals*. This *also* runs on oxygen and hydrogen and emits nothing more noxious than *water vapours*. A London-based engineering company, *Zevro*, has discovered a way of *mass-producing* these fuel cells. A suitcase-sized unit is capable of producing a kilowatt of power and the total running costs of a fuel-cell car is expected to be a *third* of the price of *petrol*.

Of course, replacing petrol-driven cars with electric or hydroelectric cars would drastically cut *pollution* levels, but it would do nothing for *traffic congestion*, or more to the point, *road deaths*. In the UK alone, there were *twenty-five million cars* on the roads in 1998, with *3,360* people being killed every year in traffic accidents. *That is a rate of ten people per day!*

A better, cleaner and more efficient form of *public transport* however, would cut down on the need for private vehicles altogether easing traffic congestion *and* road deaths. Fortunately, in 2004, London Mayor, Ken Livingston, ordered a fleet of fuel-cell buses for use on the streets of London. I remember thinking, as a teenager living in London in the fifties, that the powers-who-be were mad for getting rid of *trolleybuses* and replacing them with the diesel-powered *Routemaster* bus. Trolleybuses were *fast, efficient, clean* and *environmentally friendly*, and no *diesel* or *petrol-driven* bus could match it for *acceleration*. Why did they replace them with smelly, ugly, sluggish *diesel* buses? True, they have re-introduced *trams* in some places in Britain, but they are a poor substitute for the *trolleybus!*

One of the most *efficient* forms of public transport is the *monorail*, using the *magnetic induction* system. This uses *alternating magnets*, which push and pull in a '*wave*' motion propelling the railway along safely and efficiently at high speeds. It uses a *minimum* amount of electricity. Another advantage is that monorails either *hang* from a suspended rail *above ground* or run on *top* of it. Either way, the rails are supported at intervals by concrete support posts. This means that less ground space is used up and grass and plants can grow below the railway. Different types of monorail services have actually been operating in various parts of the world for many years.

One such supported monorail system has been operating since *1901* in the *Schwerberbahn* in *Wuppertal, Germany*, running for eight-and-a-half miles. Monorails also operate in *Tokyo*, between the airport and the downtown area; through *Darling Harbour, Sydney, Australia*; and *Dallas, Texas*, between the airport parking lot and one of the passenger terminals. Why aren't these used more extensively throughout the world?

In 1998 the Transport minister of the time, *John Prescott*, published his controversial *Integrated Transport Policy* white paper, to which I contributed. In my own report I mentioned *all* these alternative means of transport, but none were mentioned in the final paper. All he could come up with was ways of cutting down on *petrol-driven* transport! It could be that, with late twentieth century technology, such as the Internet, E-mail and TV shopping, there will be less *need* for people to travel to work and to the shops. It could even be that schoolchildren will no longer have to go to *school* but will be taught through the Internet. This would certainly cut down on private and public transport, but it would also isolate people in their own homes, leading to a society without social skills. Maybe *that* is the future of Mankind if there is any future *at all!*

Somehow we must sever this stranglehold that the oil industry has over world economy!

We must also find *renewable* resources, rather than plundering the Earth's reserves. Another way of cutting down on crude oil and petroleum would be to use *vegetable oils* as lubricants for *machinery*. Since this would come from the 'waste products' of plants, fruits and nuts (as we have already discussed in *This Garden Earth*) it would not be necessary to destroy the plants *themselves*. Indeed, because a *regular supply* would be required, this industry would actually *encourage* their growth! This would also give a boost to the agricultural and horticultural industries. Of all Mankind's activities the growing of plants, whether for commercial gain or simply for pleasure, has always been seen as the most environmentally friendly—but *is it?*

DEMON SEEDS!

I first entered the field of horticulture in 1961, after suffering a nervous breakdown. I had been working as a shipping clerk and was under a lot of stress at work, with a mortgage, etc. My doctor advised that I take an 'outdoor' job. Since I had been deeply interested in nature study, after spending my early childhood studying wildlife in the Scottish Highlands, I decided to go into horticulture. As I advanced in my new profession however, I became increasingly aware of the unwitting damage gardeners do to wildlife and the planet as a whole.

I had become aware of Mankind's damage to the environment at a very early age, as I have mentioned in previous chapters. For three years I had also

Environmentally friendly

worked as a nurse in the RAF. These various experiences, together with my growing knowledge of horticulture, gave me a unique awareness of the various aspects of the natural world around us and its intricate web of dependence one upon the other. I realised very early on in my career that the gardener's cavalier attitude towards using peat in composts and as a soil conditioner was doing the natural environment a lot of damage. I figured out too, that the increasing use of chemicals in the garden was doing far more *harm* to the environment than *good*.

I hated the idea of having to cut down trees in my job, and I came to abhor the idea of turning grassland into paved patios. I figured that the use of petrol-driven motor mowers was actually harming not only the *plants*, but also the *people* and *wildlife* in the garden. By the time I was working as a supervisor for a local landscaping firm, in the mid seventies, I caused a lot of anger from my employer by not only refusing to *use* herbicides, but also by *writing* about it in the *gardening press!* He told me that I would have to stop doing this as it could harm his business, which goes to show that he thought more of his profits than of the future of his children and grandchildren!

When I worked as Garden Steward at the Rural Studies Unit at Offley (Hertfordshire) College, my under-gardener, Jack Dovey, used to tell me stories about what gardening was like when he worked as a gardener at Drakelow Hall in the nineteen-twenties and thirties. This, too, helped me see how much things had changed for the worse during the twentieth century. In those days, before chemical weed killers and insecticides, all the weeding was done by hoe and a team of women were employed to constantly dig moss out from between the crazy paving. Horse-drawn gang mowers cut the extensive lawns and each employer was asked to collect ladybirds in a box on their way to work so they could be released into the greenhouses to eat the aphids. Much to Jack's delight I actually *introduced* the latter at Offley. It worked very well and we *never* had to use insecticides!

Another thing that people don't realise is that by putting foreign plants in our gardens we are upsetting the ecology. The great plant hunters brought these plants back from other countries at the beginning of the twentieth century. Such practices are greatly restricted nowadays and it is illegal even to dig up wild plants in *this* country and many others.

However, the damage has already been done. Many foreign plants grown in gardens have escaped, or have been deliberately planted into the wild, wreaking havoc with our own native flora. The *Japanese* Knotweed and the Giant Hogweed from the Caucasias, for example, have run rampant in parts of the British Isles. The *Spanish* Bluebell, larger and more robust than our *native* Bluebell have escaped from gardens and crossed with the British version and is practically hybridising it out of existence.

What we must remember is that plants can escape into the wild in many ways. Some British woods are full of snowdrops. Now snowdrops are not native to this country, although many people are under the impression that they are because so many are found in the wild. The fact is that they grow on the sites of long-forgotten monasteries. They remained long after all evidence of the old monastery gardens had gone. Also some people mistakenly believe they are adding to the wealth of our countryside by deliberately planting other plants, whilst other plants escape via seed unwittingly distributed by birds, animals and the wind. This is what I call the 'demon seed' syndrome. This is happening with *many* of our native flora. They are becoming extinct in the face of competition from more robust *foreign* species, or from varieties that have been especially raised by plant breeders.

Another real problem is with *genetically engineered* plants. Genetic engineering began in horticulture and agriculture in the nineteen fifties, when it was discovered that the genetic material of cells could be altered with the use of chemicals such as colchicine and digitalin, or by bombardment with radiation. Since then genetic engineering has become big business, not only in plants but also in the livestock farming industry. Again, there is a danger that genetically altered plants can cross with the native flora rendering the endemic plants extinct, but there are even *greater* problems here.

Plants are altered genetically for many commercial reasons. Not only can it produce bigger and more robust plants, but it can also create plants that are resistant to diseases, fungal attacks, pests, and even weedkillers! The problems here are that if, for example, a genetically-engineered cereal crop crosses naturally with one of our *native* grasses, then that grass will *also* be resistant to diseases, etc. The idea of making a food plant resistant to *herbicides* is so that a whole field can be sprayed and, in theory, the surrounding weeds should die, leaving the crop intact. Nobody, however, explains what happens to *us* when we *eat* the crop!

There are problems too when plants are genetically altered to produce *pest-resistant* crops. In nineteen ninety-eight it was discovered that ladybirds were becoming sterile after eating aphids that had fed on some of these pest-resistant crops. If, as a result, ladybirds became extinct through this practice there would be plagues of aphids such as blackfly and greenfly, because they would have no natural predators!

It is my belief that many chemicals used in horticulture and agriculture, whether used in sprays or in the creation of genetically engineered plants, are affecting the reproductive systems of *many* creatures—including Mankind. Radiation too, whether used in the genetics industry or, as became fashionable in the nineteen-nineties, to preserve fruit and vegetables, is affecting the sperm count in male humans.

THE LEMMING FACTOR

We add preservatives and colouring to our food such as *Aspartame*, which is known to cause severe headaches and even brain haemorrhage. This is found in *Diet Coke* and indeed, in most sugar-free drinks and foods and is the basis of sugar substitutes such as *Canderel*, *Splendor* and *Spoonful*. The truth is that this artificial sweetener is more harmful to your health than sugar itself! Many artificial colourings in food, such as *Sudan dyes*, which are added to food such as pre-packaged curries and chilli dishes to make them look red and fiery, are actually *poisons*—and yet these and other dyes are still added to our food, despite the dangers to health.

Many food additives have been linked to personality disorders and hyperactivity in children. Modern 'fast-foods' such as burgers, which originated in The United States, are not only full of these additives, but also fat, sinew and even skin and feathers, which normally, humans would not eat. The commercial reason for this, of course, is that the more of the animal or poultry that is used in the burger, the more profit the company makes. The result is that, certainly in the case of poultry, the whole bird is ground down into a 'mush' that is eventually made into a burger. Because of this, and lack of exercise through going everywhere by car we, and our children, are becoming obese and prone to heart disorders. Perhaps this is part of the human 'lemming factor' and that we are subconsciously bringing about our own extinction!

REDISTRIBUTION OF WILDLIFE

Ever since Mankind learned to travel from continent to continent he has, either wittingly or unwittingly, redistributed fauna as well as flora across the globe, often with disastrous results. It began, as we have discussed previously, with mice and rats stowing away on ships. Of course, smaller creatures such as fleas, lice and bacteria and viruses have been distributed in this way too—in the hair, skin, clothing and breath of the travellers. In order to combat the problem of rats and mice Mankind has taken cats on voyages with him, with disastrous results for the local wildlife. For companionship he has also taken with him dogs, parrots and other pets and at other times he has introduced goats, pigs, cattle, etc., for food.

Many people probably regard the rabbit as indigenous to The British Isles and Europe, but this is not so. The Romans originally discovered that rabbits were a good source of food when they invaded North Africa, so they took some back to Rome in the 12th Century, where they were bred for their fur and as food. From there, the Romans introduced them to all their outposts, including Britain, where, due to their amazing breeding ability and changes to agricultural practices, they rapidly began to outnumber our two native species of indigenous hare (the brown hare and the blue or mountain hare) by the beginning of the 20th Century. Between 1919 and the 1950s British Farmers deliberately introduced the rabbit disease *myxomatosis* in order to eradicate what had, in his eyes, become a 'pest'.

Young people may be forgiven for believing that the grey squirrel is also native to the UK because of their abundance, but this, again, is completely untrue. Unlike our native red squirrel it is actually an American tree rat, and was introduced into the UK at the end of the nineteenth century. By the 1970s, it had replaced the native red squirrel by 46%, as well as causing untold damage to forests and woodland by stripping tree bark during the winter. The grey squirrel is much more robust than the red squirrel and as a result our indigenous species simply couldn't put up with the competition. The threat to the native squirrel became so severe that during the forties 'bounty hunters' were actually paid one shilling for every grey squirrel tail they could produce!

More recently, through quicker air travel, scorpions have made themselves at home in a railway station in Surrey, whilst 125 alien species of spider have made themselves at home in Britain, including some poisonous ones. At Christmas 2005 Jan Price fled her home in Gorslas, South Wales after a creature 'the size of a CD' was eventually identified as a bird-eating spider from Nepal. Apparently, it had hitched a ride in her knapsack whilst she had been on holiday there! The most dangerous spider discovered so far in Britain, by The Government's Central Science Laboratory, is the highly poisonous Melbourne trapdoor spider, which measures 3.5 cm across and whose poison is lethal. So what can we do in order to make amends for all these mistakes?

NEW CENTURY RESOLUTIONS!

Before the twenty-first century gets too old we must make resolutions to help the planet and that means, if we are to have any impact at this late stage, changing our whole outlook on life as well as our whole lifestyle.

The biggest single factor in global warming is the use of petrol, which, as I have already said, should have been left in the ground in the first place, but now that we are drilling for it, why should we continue to rely upon it? Some may argue that you cannot simply stop people using their cars, but look how much unnecessary pollution we cause throughout the world by motor racing! Banning the use of cars and motorbikes merely for sporting purposes should be a priority for *any* government. After all, there *are* alternatives to petrol, including electric cars, fuel cells and solar-powered vehicles. Interestingly, more electric vehicles are produced in the UK than in any other country in the world. Unfortunately, they are almost entirely made up of milk floats and golf buggies. But we have the technology and if manufacturers can produce electric vehicles for commercial reasons and for the sporting gentry, why can't they produce cheap electric vehicles for the masses? The main thing that puts people off electric, fuel cell or hybrid vehicles is the cost—and yet there is no reason at all why these vehicles cannot be sold at the same price as petrol-powered vehicles. The only thing preventing this is that they dare not upset the oil companies and therefore the world economy by making alternative vehicles as cheap as petrol-driven ones!

We could stop importing plants and animals into foreign countries, ban all horticultural and agricultural chemicals and we should call a halt to *all* genetic engineering.

We should also have respect for all living things and ban zoos, intensive farming, working animals and pets and we should concentrate more on protecting our own native species.

It is the use of chemicals such as pesticides, plus the general pollution of the air and waters of Earth and the destruction of natural habitat, that has led to the rapid decline of once common birds. In Britain alone the *house sparrow*, once one of the *commonest* of our native birds, is now a *protected species!* In the past twenty-five years its population has *halved!* The turtledove, a favourite of poets over the centuries, has declined by 75% in twenty-five years to only 75,000. The skylark too, has seen its population decline by 75% over the same period.

Native British *animals* that have seen a disastrous fall in their population include the *red squirrel* (halved in 25 years); *water vole* (75% reduction); the *otter* (30% drop in population); the *pipistrelle bat* (reduced from 6 million to 2 million); the *harvest mouse* (population halved to 1.5 million); and the *common frog*, which has been hit by deformities and an alarming drop in population.

Amongst British *insects* the all-essential *honeybee* and *bumblebee* are decreasing rapidly and the *mole cricket*, once very common in Britain, has seen its population drop from *millions* to only a *handful*.

We could use the *basic ingredients* of peat rather than the peat *itself*, which has taken millions of years for nature to produce. By basic ingredients I am talking, again, about renewable resources such as leaf mould, the crumbling wood of rotted trees and tree bark. Like our forefathers I have been using these materials for years. At Offley in the 1960s I regularly gathered rotted tree bark from the woods and used it as compost and mulch and I have been making my own compost and using farm manure for many years. This ensures that our natural peat bogs remain intact and to hell with the big peat companies! I have used *many* substitutes for peat over the years, including spent hops from a brewery and spent compost from a mushroom farm, when I worked in the Parks Department at Blackpool, Lancashire. Another good substitute is *Coir*, or coconut fibre, now available from most garden centres.

We should call a halt to the mining of metals and other minerals. Precious stones and metals such as *silver* and *gold* have very little *practical* use. They are used purely for decoration and as status symbols. True, *gold* is used in the production of *catalytic converters*, which are of very little use in cutting down car emissions *anyway! Industrial diamonds* can be manufactured using *carbon*, whilst *pearls*, one of nature's *waste* products should only be used as a spin-off from the *seafood industry*. I feel sure that Mankind could easily do without his diamond, ruby and emerald necklaces and rings. Even wedding and engagement rings are an unnecessary leftover of Man's primitive needs. Like the anklets and bracelets worn by slaves, such rings are merely a sign that the wearer is the property of the person who gave it to them. It is yet another sign of Mankind's greed. I am sure that this view will outrage moralists and religious groups, but then I expect various passages of this book have upset just about *everyone* in some way or another! It really doesn't *matter* to me all I am concerned about is the welfare of the planet as a whole.

We could outlaw all blood sports, the fur and ivory trade, as well as the hunting of rhinos for the supposed 'aphrodisiac' properties of their horns. Let's face it the biggest turn-on of all is to live upon a beautiful planet, which is rich in myriads of life forms.

Crocodiles and alligators could be saved from extinction by banning the trade in skins for shoes and handbags. Exotic birds could be left to live in peace by banning the trade in feathers for clothes and hats, unless, of course, they are obtained from the natural *moulting* process.

The practice of trapping animals, birds, reptiles and fish for the pet trade and for zoos, circuses and street photographers could also be banned without any drastic effects upon the world economy—much better to allow animals to live in their natural surroundings, protected by adequate laws. The only forms of 'zoo' should be in the form of wildlife parks, comprising of thousands of acres, where animals could roam in safety from the greed of Mankind. Even then animals should *not* be made to live in countries that are not their native homes. Animals have evolved to exist in certain locations, with specific environmental conditions. Polar bears are not happy in temperate regions, for they have adapted to *arctic* conditions. Likewise lions are only happy in *tropical* environments. Once we have set about righting the wrongs we have done to the environment we should make sure these animals live their lives as nature intended, *in their own environment.*

Many *plants too* are adapted to particular conditions. What is the point in keeping tropical plants in a *hothouse in Britain,* for example, when they would be far happier in their *native climes*? This is as bad as keeping *birds* in an *aviary and fish in bowls and aquariums!* Hopefully, by the middle of this century these practices will be deemed as barbaric as stuffing and mounting animals and sticking butterflies on boards with pins!

I am a trained horticulturist and have grown many plants as a part of my job and for my own pleasure. I have grown alpine plants from the high Alps and I have grown tropical plants in glasshouses—but do we do this out of love for the *plants*? I'm afraid *not*. Like so-called *pet-lovers*, we do it purely for our *own* pleasure or profit. Fortunately, I have been able to see beyond my own passion and I would like other gardeners to at least consider my point of view.

Our *monorail systems* could allow people to view and photograph animals and plants in safety for the human observers and without too much interference to the natural balance of the wildlife parks. The *greatest* plus would be that there would be no exposure of pollution to either the animals or the plants.

Forests and woodlands, swamps and bogs, marshes, meadows, in fact any places where rare and threatened species still survive, should be left *strictly undisturbed* as nature intended. Householders should be encouraged to plant 'wildlife gardens' on their own land. Local councils should be encouraged to leave natural sites alone and create 'green spaces' within the boundaries of our towns and cities. They could also be encouraged to replant *native* flora in the surrounding countryside.

There should be stricter laws covering plant collecting from the wild. Already in the UK the lady's slipper orchid, *cyprepedium calceolous,* has been dug up from the wild to the very edge of extinction, whilst such uniquely British plants such as the oxlip, *primula elatior,* the snakes head fritillary, *fritillaria meleagris,* the snowflakes, the pasque flower and several *less spectacular* British wild plants are fast disappearing from our countryside. The mass looting of wild plants is a hugely profitable industry throughout the world. In Turkey eleven species of crocus and four types of cyclamen are fast disappearing. The dog's-tooth violet, *erythronium dens-canis* is becoming extinct in western Europe, whilst in France and Turkey wild populations of the common snowdrop are under threat of total extinction due to indiscriminate plant-hunters. The *reticulata iris* now only grows wild on *one* lonely mountain in Georgia, in the former USSR. Even there it is fast disappearing. *Most* rare species of plants are now grown in nurseries and sold through reputable nurserymen, but the illegal trade still goes on.

It is often much cheaper to buy plants that have been dug up from the wild by starving peasants than it is to buy them from a commercial nursery—and many travellers do this, *despite* heavy penalties in many countries throughout the world. A few years ago *Henry Azadhedel* was found to have 348 wild orchids with him when he returned from his travels. 334 of these were protected species. He was jailed for twelve months; eight of them suspended, and fined £10,000. On the open market these would have fetched £42,000!

Perhaps we could plant more forests and woodlands in order to supply *this Garden Earth* with more oxygen and to take up more carbon dioxide. This would help to put right some of the damage Mankind has already done. True, *The National Forest Project* (on which I am a consultant) is *already* doing this in the UK, but at the same time the government is insisting upon destroying thousands of acres of green belt land, and other areas of countryside, for the building of housing estates! Hardly makes sense, does it?

Above all Mankind *must* come to realise that nature knows no boundaries. It does not recognise fences, walls, or the boundaries drawn up by Mankind to divide the land into different countries. An earthquake, for example, could rip through Israel, Palestine, Saudi Arabia, Kuwait, Iraq and Iran, without stopping to consider religious or political boundaries. Indeed, the Kashmir earthquake of 2005 ripped through the borders between India and Pakistan bringing those people closer together in a common cause than they had been for centuries!

As far as *nature* is concerned a species of advanced apes, which choose to call themselves Mankind share *This Garden Earth* with billions of *other* species—and we are only here with nature's *consent*. Not by the grace of *God*, but by the grace of the *planet!*

It would be great if Mankind could actually learn a lesson from all of this, the result of a lifetime's study, and come to realise that we are all inhabitants of the same planet. We should all live together in harmony and peace, not only with *each other* but also with *all* our fellow inhabitants, whether they are animal, vegetable and, yes, even *mineral*. We are *all* a part of the planet that I call '*This Garden Earth*'.

Finally, we should all come to realise that if there *is* a God, he would not only represent all races of Mankind but all species of life upon this planet. I believe that God is the Power of Nature. It is responsible for our very existence and for the existence of the planet on which we live as well as the *entire universe*, which we are not even *close* to understanding. Why, even *religious organizations* that preach we should respect *God's creation* actually *destroy* that creation by building churches on God's land. Then they go and add insult to injury by building *car parks* for the patrons, encouraging the *pollution* of God's creation! What hypocrisy! I mentioned this at a meeting of the Real World Alliance in 2001. The Committee was made up of representatives from the Quakers, the Roman Catholic Church, the Church of England and the Baha'i faith. My comments were met with stunned silence until the chairman, himself a Quaker, told the committee, "I think Mr Perry is absolutely right, we must *all* take responsibility for the state of the Earth…"

If there were not any *religious* or *political* barriers then we could all get on with the business of living in peace and harmony with the rest of creation—a 'brotherhood of the earth', which cares about all living things and for the planet which spawned us. This is what the late *John Lennon* was saying when he wrote '*Imagine*'. Very few people listened to *him*—why should *I* be any *different*? Even so I couldn't leave *This Garden Earth* without *trying!*

Mind you, in November 2001, former Government Chief Scientist, *Lord May,* warned that animal and plant species are now disappearing 1,000 times faster than would normally be expected.

Blaming deforestation, technology, pollution and human greed, he was reported as saying, "There is little doubt we are standing on the breaking tip of the sixth great wave of extinction in the history of life on Earth. We have more land under intensive cultivation, which gets us closer to realizing the dream of agriculture since its dawn. That is to grow crops no other creature eats except us, but not shared with weeds or insects, which we regard as pests." Perhaps he should have read these two volumes, *This Garden Earth* and *Vandals in The Garden*, which have been three decades in the researching and writing!

He admitted experts have said that 1.5 million known creatures have become extinct over the past century. The previous five mass extinctions, starting 440 million years ago, were caused by *natural* disasters. The *current* wave of extinction began 10,000 years ago, when Mankind began to dominate the planet. Royal Society President, *Lord May*, was speaking at London's *Natural History Museum* and finished by saying, "This current bout of extinction is definitely being caused by us." *It's a pity he didn't admit all this when he was working for the Government!*

Only when mankind as a species realises these things, and does something about it, will we have reached the stage where we could *truly* call ourselves mature and worthy of the title, '*The Caretakers of the Planet*'. Unfortunately, as a species we still have an awful lot of 'growing up' to do before we leave behind us our destructive 'teenage years'. I could never have continued with my lifetime's work if I had not been the eternal optimist and I still believe that one day, when most of us have finally reached maturity as a species and learned to respect the planet on which we live, as well as all its living creatures, we will forever be able to shed the title, *Vandals in the Garden*. Until then I shall continue '*crying for the Earth*'.

Note: If you want to find ways of turning every city, town and village into a more environmentally-friendly one, visit my website www.geocities.com/widgeripoo and go to *The World of Pete Perry*, where you will be able to access our environmental pages. Here you can find everything from fuel cell cars, through wind and solar power units to complete monorail systems.

Further Reading: . . . . *This Garden Earth*
Coming soon: . . . . *The Garden Fights Back!*